# May I Help You Understand?

**Also Written By Darrell D. Simms**
    "Black Experience, Strategies & Tactics In The Business World"

**Also Published By Management Aspects Inc.**
"For My Peoples" by Shanisse R. Howard

# May I Help You Understand?

*"Information To Improve Racial And Cultural Relations*
*Between White And Black Americans"*

## A Sustainable Community Development Approach

### By Darrell D. Simms

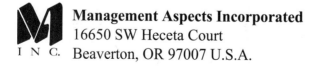

**Management Aspects Incorporated**
16650 SW Heceta Court
Beaverton, OR 97007 U.S.A.

# May I Help You Understand?

*"Information To Improve Racial and Cultural Relations Between White and Black Americans"*

## A Sustainable Community Development Approach
### By Darrell D. Simms

Published by:

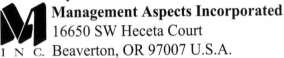 **Management Aspects Incorporated**
16650 SW Heceta Court
I N C. Beaverton, OR 97007 U.S.A.

**Copyright** @ 1999 by Darrell D. Simms
First Printing $16.95

**Library of Congress Cataloging-in-Publication Data**
Simms, Darrell, 1999
    May I help you understand? : information to improve
racial and cultural relations between white and black
Americans : a sustainable community development
approach / by Darrell D. Simms. – 1st ed.
       p. cm.
    Includes bibliographical references and index.
     ISBN: 0-9630776-7-8
     1. United States—Race relations. 2. Afro-Americans—
History. 3. Afro-Americans—Attitudes. 4. Racism—
United States. I. Title
E185.61.S56 1999
305.8'96073                   QBI98-1469
                                   CIP

# About The Author

Born in New Orleans, Louisiana, on May 31, 1953, Darrell Simms spent his formative years living in government project housing. He attended school inconsistently, finally dropping out at the age of 14 to work as a caddy at the nearby country club. After finding his way back to school and inspired by his step-mother to do something worthwhile with his life, at age 19 he enlisted in the navy, which provided him with a chance for a college education under the GI bill.

After a Navy tour in the Philippines, he entered the University of Washington through the assistance of an Equal Opportunity Program. He ended up in a Physics research program that was design to find better methods for teaching educationally disadvantaged minorities. This led him to discover a love for Physics where he was able to excel academically. He graduated with a minor in Physics and a BS in Industrial Engineering. His academic achievements continued, and, years later, he taught a management class at the University of Oregon's Graduate School of Management for several years.

After graduation, Darrell became a nuclear power safety engineer for Westinghouse, a technical salesman for IBM and an executive assistant to the city council for the City of Portland Oregon. At this time, he noticed how inequitably and poorly people work and communicate with each other from different ethnic backgrounds, especially Black and White Americans. In the navy and at the university, he had learned he could understand people from different ethnic backgrounds, especially White Americans. As his understanding grew, he developed a fascination with interracial relations and a desire to share his insight with others.

This desire was realized in 1990 when he started Management Aspects Incorporated (MA, Inc.) The mission of the firm is to help organizations to understand racial, ethnic, and cultural issues, in addition to helping them manage organizational change. Extending Darrell's previous work for the City of Portland, MA, Inc. has assisted government municipalities in developing minority- and women-owned businesses. Combining his Christian faith with interracial understanding, he has worked with churches to help them improve interracial understanding.

In 1991, Darrell Simms published "Black Experience, Strategies & Tactics in The Business World," a book written to assist young, professional Black Americans to succeed in corporate America. He has also authored a curriculum for helping to teach management and organizational development to help improve racial and cultural relations to many northwest organizations and corporations. Through his community involvement he co-founded Project MISTER, a program to encourage young Black men to take responsibility for their lives in Seattle, Washington.

Darrell lives with his wife of 21 years, Nelda, and his children, Darsha and Thorin in Beaverton, Oregon.

# Acknowledgements

This book was written to enhance the lives of people who should dare to read it, but it represents the education I have received from the people I have had the opportunity to live, work and play with and to you all, I say thank you very much! Many thanks go to my grammatical editor Patricia Griffiths who can make my writing come alive and comprehendible by the most intellectual of readers. Leslie White of DP Printing provided invaluable consultation to the project.

I have many friends who listened to my ideas over the last two years. Most of you are glad the book is done so you don't have to listen to the conversation that always seemed to steer to the topics of this book. I want to express many thanks to Tyrone and Cyndy Henry, John and Pat Griffiths, Steve Hanamura, Johnnie and Cheri Thomas, Fred and Vera Cliff. Also thanks to Mike and Debbie Sloane, Betty Dillon, Joe Savola and Gayle Martinez for taking the time to give the book such a great final read.

I must always acknowledge that wonderful lady who continues to listen, comment and inspire my life, my mother, Ellenese Brooks Simms and also my father Melvin Simms.

Finally, I want to thank my wife Nelda and my children Darsha and Thorin for the time they let me take away from them and put towards these passions of mine. Passions, that I am sure they hope will finally reap some return on our investments we have made in these projects.

Special acknowledgement to Tim Bacon who challenged me to use my God given skills and talents to help make the world a better place for all of us. Many thanks to Pastor Clark Tanner and the entire Beaverton Christian Church family for their sustaining support and encouragement through this project.

## Dedicated

*To my Sisters: Carol, Majesta, Cynthia, Patricia, Karen, Ganelle, Diane, Stacy, Debra, and Christelle.*

*To my brothers: Melvin, Gregory, Kenneth, Dwight, Shannon and Bobbie.*

*To the Almighty God who made America the beautiful for all of us.*

# Contents

# Who Should Read This Book

*This book should be read by all who are committed to the continued improvement of life in America for all the people that have come to be an American.*

*For those of you who think White Americans are some how better than Black Americans, this book should help you realize you have somehow been misguided and misinformed about Black Americans.*

*To those of you who call yourselves Promise Keepers, you will truly want to walk through the pages of this book and work hard to understand the information presented here.*

*For those of you who make decisions about peoples' lives in corporate America, you will find this book very helpful when it comes to assimilating Black Americans into the hollow halls of your businesses and its practices.*

*And most of all, to those of you who have been told by Black Americans, "You Don't Understand!"*

# Introduction

One of the biggest problems America has ever faced in its History looms large on its horizon. It has already decimated the people native to this land. It's a problem that continues to rise and set with the sun each and everyday of our lives for those of us who call ourselves American. That problem is called **Racial Enmity**. It exists between all the races, but appears to be most destructive for the relations of Black and White America. This problem finds its components in our inability to find equality and equitable opportunities for all that choose to live in this country. It is a most simple problem, yet it appears so complex to most of us. The wall seems to grow like a self-perpetuating cloud that often covers and obscures all of the success we have experienced in this country to date. In America we are problem solvers and any problem we set out to solve, we always find a **solution**. We must make the resolution of this problem a priority in our society, in our economy, in our government, and in each and every one of our lives. I am confident as an American that we will solve this problem, if we first take time to understand each other's wants, needs and dreams.

I believe America is ready to solve this problem. I believe America has finally matured enough to take on a problem that its people fear is virtually unsolvable. At the time of authorship William Clinton is president and his administration is convinced that race relations is a key problem for the nation to solve. He kicked off a year long Initiative on Race – One America. The Clinton Administration set five goals for the country:

1. Set a vision of racial reconciliation and a just and unified America.
2. Educate the nation about the facts surrounding the issue of race.
3. Promote constructive dialogue, to confront and work through the difficult and controversial issues surrounding race.
4. Recruit and encourage leadership at all levels to help bridge racial divides.

5. Find, develop and implement solutions in critical areas such as education, economic opportunity, housing, health care, crime and the administration of justice – for individuals, communities, corporations and governments at all levels.

None of these goals seem to be lofty goals, in fact, I think the President and his administration have set their sights a bit too low. At this time in America we have one of the best, sustained economies we have ever experienced in our history. We have the lowest overall unemployment rate ever and people are in a good mood to do well. The quality of life has become a high priority for Americans.

I first got the idea to write this book after watching a series of shows hosted by Ted Koppel on the program called "Nightline." The series was entitled **America in Black and White** initially a weeklong show and has been on-going for several years. I applauded Ted Koppel and the ABC Television Network for devoting initially, five hours and hence, five nights to this crucial topic, my only regret was that it wasn't broadcast during prime time. The show was unique in that it presented several different viewpoints from several different vantagepoints. Add the commentation and facilitation of Ted Koppel and it became award winning.

Ted Koppel is one of my favorite news commentators because of his ability to make me feel he is genuinely interested in the topics he chooses to moderate. In presenting this topic, I do believe he found the topic that is on the minds of Americans more today, than any of us would like to admit. Anyway, I was watching the show and what moved me more than any other part of the show was a White gentleman, who I believe was a minister, commenting on a discussion he was observing via a monitor as Ted facilitated. The discussion that was being observed, on the monitor, was a group of Black people discussing all of the racial injustice they had experienced in their lives and this discussion was also being facilitated by Ted. (The wonders of television.) The minister said something that I had heard stated by many of my

# Introduction

White colleagues in corporate America, many of the White MBA students I taught at the University of Oregon and many other Whites I have encountered or observed throughout my life. He said, "Blacks always tells us, **YOU DON'T UNDERSTAND**." "You don't understand the Black Experience in America; you don't understand what Blacks have to go through to be Black in America." (Inflexion: It would be hard to understand all the negative experiences that are brought about simply because of the color of ones skin.) I believe right about that time, I heard something that has always plagued many of our relationships in society and our relationships throughout the world. Somebody wanted to understand and nobody took on the challenge of the request of helping him or her to understand. Now, before all you Black Americans start clamoring and complaining about how many times you have tried to make White Americans understand, keep reading a while longer. Besides, the book was not written for you, it was written for my fellow White Americans like Ted and the many other White Americans that are truly trying to understand the plight of Black Americans. How to make America a better place to live for all people.

The other motivation for writing this book: On June 3, 1996, I was in Algiers, a little community on the west bank of the Mississippi River in New Orleans, Louisiana, my home town where I grew up as a kid. Algiers a once poor, but thriving community for Black folk. I never realized how poor until this particular day. I was driving around trying to find a bank cash machine and I stopped a young Black man to ask for help. I asked the young man, "where is the nearest bank?" He looked at me with great surprise, a quizzical look and answered, "A bank! In Algiers!" He then explained to me that I needed to go up near the Algiers Ferry Dock to the Whitney Bank. And then it dawned on me, oh yes, the Whitney Bank. That was the only bank in all of Algiers when I was a kid. When I got to the Whitney Bank, there was no cash machine. I was overwhelmed with my situation and that there was no cash machine in this predominantly African American community. Now, I travel all over the country and I never give any thought to not being able to find a cash machine, let alone a bank. This reminded me from which America I have come from and that there is still work for me to do in making this world a better place for all people. By the way, I found a cash machine in an area of town that mainly house White residents, about five miles away. I immediately pulled out my tape recorder and captured this experience to relate to the audience of this book.

This book hopes to take on the challenge of helping White Americans understand some things about Black Americans. I am convinced, if I can bring about some understanding between the White Culture in America and the Black Culture in America, I have done a good thing. These two cultures will continue to struggle to live together in America as long as they do not understand each other. They will never fully gain the trust needed to continue to forge the American culture, which continues to be a fragmented culture based on this lack of understanding. I know if we can bring about more understanding, we will continue to make progress between these two races of people who call themselves Americans. If I simply make you stop and think, as you pursue this understanding, I will count this book a major success. If it makes White and Black Americans understand each other a little better than they did before reading it, I have accomplished a great mission I undertook in life many years ago: Helping Americans enhance the quality of their lives!

I do not dare think this will be an exhaustive piece of work. If you choose to read this book, it might generate more questions than answers. I would at least hope it generates a much more positive dialogue than we have had so far. As I write this section, you should know that I am smiling. As I wrote this book, you should know that I smiled a lot. To those of you who are White, the smile makes you think that I might be cordial and this book might have some positive significance. For those of you that are Black, the smile might make you think, there is something not quite right here and I hope this brother don't misrepresent us. Historically, the smile has been something not to be trusted by Black Americans, especially when White Americans were doing the smiling.

# Introduction

The smile is a gesture in culture that has different interpretations by the different ethnicities that make up the American culture. The smile is a place to start trying to understand each other: Such a simple gesture that is often devastatingly misinterpreted. This book attempts to explain such simple differences that have been so divisive between the American people.

We must clearly gain an understanding about how different we are and also how much alike we all are, if we are ever to understand who we are in America. We are different and different for the most part has been proclaimed bad when it comes to race. We work so hard at building one America and that should be the task. But the whole is only as good as the sum of its parts. I have a claim and that claim is, "to be different is to be American." We all believe this, but we have a hard time promoting this. How ironic for a country founded on liberty and justice for all, which both have their foundation embedded in allowing people to be whatever they want to be.

This book only attempts to deal with ethnic and relational differences between no one other than Black and White Americans at this writing. Please do not go through the book wondering why I didn't include Asians or Hispanics or Native Americans or even Women. I was always taught to put my own house in order before I go trying to help clean up someone else's. I truly believe that only the people who live a set of experiences can truly convey to another people how to understand their true perspective on their lives as Americans. And, I would not dare try and steal the thunder of my other ethnic counterparts. I wanted to be a bit selfish for the Black race of Americans and present a case that is often drawn attention to, but then pushed aside in the name of other ethnic minorities. Black Americans still seem to reap the smallest benefit that they often fought for in this great American country.

I am one who believes Americans are the greatest people on earth. Why? America makes room for all people who dare to call it home. But the process (assimilation) that makes it great, absorbs the essences of what makes cultures beautiful, into what is now a majority culture and ends up being guilty of destroying what it was set up to protect. Historically, Black Americans entered the process unwillingly and the process has failed to be fair due to the ineffectiveness of the process to get pass the color of our skin. For Black Americans, it has been a progressive tearing of the culture and a constant losing of hope, with the blame falling on those who have benefited from the process the most, White Americans.

You White Americans of this modern day time have inherited a very monumental problem: Racism. As large of a problem as it is, I am confident that you are more than capable of helping fix it. I will be the first to standup and say you are not to be blamed for this problem. But, you inherited the house and with the house come all of the assets, liabilities and responsibilities. You are now responsible for what happens in this house as an owner of the house. A house that you have shared the occupancy with Black Americans for centuries. You must now share the ownership with us. You are a diligent and decided people and you can do anything you set your minds to do. I am confident that you and I will continue to repair this wonderful house called America, the land of the free and the brave. I don't believe I have to remind you that it is not a land of the free until everyone is free! When everyone is free, then and only then will you be relieved of this burden that was past down by your foreparents. I am ready to continue the work to repair this house. The structure is built on a solid foundation and the beauty is already there to be enjoyed by all. Let's get to work!

I do challenge all Americans to keep asking us Black Americans to help make you understand who we are and what we are all about. I challenge all Black Americans to work hard at making White Americans understand that we really are who we say we are. After all, there is one thing we should all understand, we are one nation under God indivisible and we all stand for liberty and justice for all. I believe we are all still in that same boat.

# Chapter
# 1

## Didn't We Come Over On The Same Boat, Just On Different Decks: A Historical Perspective?

*B*lack people and White people came to America on the same boats at the same time. White people were on the passenger decks; Black people were in the cargo holds. This is not being stated to place blame on any person, place, or thing. It is simply a set of important facts that is part of our American history. In America we have chosen history as the basis for our beliefs. Our beliefs provide the basis for our lives, enabling us to assimilate new facts usefully so we can better shape our future.

Sidebar - Opinion: There is some confusion as to whether the people in America with so-called "black" skin are to be called Black people or people of African descent. Do we refer to these people in America as African Americans or Black Americans? They are both correct! I think we can all agree, most of the Americans with so-called white skin are of European descent. We, in America do not call them European Americans or more correct German Americans, Italian Americans, Irish Americans or Russian Americans, etc. We simply call them White Americans or just plain Americans. I have taken the liberty in this book to use BLACK AMERICANS to refer to the people in America with Black skin and claim America as their home country. End Sidebar

The information in this chapter will present information on the origin of Black people and how they became Black Americans through a long and arduous journey through American history.

# Chapter 1

## *What Is This History Black Americans Seem To Cling To?*

America is a country that lives in tradition, heritage, and assimilation. Although assimilation erases a lot of history for Americans of all ethnic backgrounds, it continues to serves as a reminder to Black Americans of their historic plight and long journey to become "true Americans." Being true Americans means being able to take advantage of the opportunities available to all Americans, but opportunities that mainly seem to benefit White Americans.

Black and White Americans got off to a perfectly bad start, as you will see from this historical perspective. Until the late 1950's, Black Americans were taught you are not a people. This teaching inflicted wounds so deep that they have not yet healed.

One result of these wounds was to hinder them in finding their place in America. Ironically, as slaves, Black Americans knew their place in America, even if it was a bad place. Once that place was taken away from them, for all the right reasons, they were lost in America. Even today, we struggle to find our place in the American culture, a culture that we can call our own. So we attempt to adopt the African culture. Many Blacks might disagree, but trying to adopt the African culture is even harder than trying to assimilate into the American culture. We Black Americans know so little about the African culture and, thanks to the media, we mostly see the negative side of the rich African culture. We have latched onto some of the physical aspects of African culture, such as kente cloth and dread locks. Yes, this is confusing! The question "Who am I?" is very important to the Black American, because it makes us wonder if we have no culture to call our own. So we choose a weapon that other races have used for thousands of years to validate their culture, and that weapon is history!

Don't underestimate the power of history as a weapon! If you read the Bible or any other historical writing, you will see people killing one another to protect their value systems, their beliefs and culture. Rarely, in the beginning, is the battle over wealth. Most of the battles were fought to assimilate the other cultures into the dominating or conquering culture. Most of the Holy wars were fought over beliefs and traditions. Early Christians also clung to their beliefs despite repression, as do Christians in some non-western cultures today. The Jews, although repressed while in Egypt, risked death to serve God. The Muslim nations continue to fight for what they believe and practice. The day I wrote this chapter, Sadam Hussein tried to beat the Kurdish factions into submission. Sadam should know, history allows us to create what we need based on passed experiences. A people who fight to protect their beliefs, fight to the death. Like the Kurds, the Black American culture is alive and well, but the tension between our culture and the mainstream American culture continues.

Black Americans add the spice of our culture in a variety of areas, seeking to balance cultural integration with maintaining our own identity. From Afros to fades. From dashikis to collarless shirts. From Black southern dialects to northeastern Jersey jive talk. During the workday we speak the textbook English, but outside work we speak the dialect of the Black American culture.

An important element of this cultural tension is the fact that the Black transition to full equality is still in process. This continues to confuse us as a country, affecting both Whites and Blacks. Music is one example of this confusion. Many Whites love Black music. Kenny G. is White, but he plays his saxophone in a very soulful Black Style. Joe Cocker sings in what we Blacks would call a crooning style. Charlie Pride is Black but he sings in a country style. More White Americans attend jazz festivals than Blacks do, even though Black Americans created jazz. Winton and Brandon Marsalis draw more Whites to their concerts than Blacks. Michael Jackson continues to sell tapes and CD's to Whites and Blacks. Not only is he accepted nationally, he has transcended more cultures and peoples internationally than any other musician of our time. Ironically, Michael continues to try to change his appearance, looking less Black with each surgery, but his looks don't sell his music, his dancing and singing does. His Black heritage, specifically his background in gospel singing and Motown, has been vital to his success.

The best place to eat in the United States is New Orleans. The New Orleans chefs are mostly Black. Those that are White learned to cook as the Black New Orleans chefs do. Here is an example of how interdependent Blacks and Whites have become on one another. I have a White friend who grew up in the San Francisco Bay Area, and spent a considerable amount of time in Oakland, a predominantly Black community. When he first moved to Beaverton, Oregon, he said he felt culturally deprived because there weren't many Black people. He asked me where all the Black people were. I replied, down in Oakland where you left them. We both laughed.

Black Americans have a proud and rich heritage, dating back four hundred years. Alex Haley gave us a great snap shot of this beginning in his best selling book, "Roots." Through it, America saw how Black people happened to arrive in America. The movie "Roots" was as educational for Black Americans as it was for White Americans. It was eye opening to see how America was built. Let's recap the basic facts of where Black Americans came from, how they arrived in America, and what some of their experiences in America have been, how they helped build America.

### *What Are The Basics Of Black American History?*

### Where Did Black People Come From?

Understanding where Black people came from is a good basis to better understand Black Americans.

Sidebar: Several books were used to develop this discussion: The African Origin of Civilization, by Cheikh Anta Diop, Lawrence Hill and Company, 1974; The Great Fear, edited by Gary B. Nash and Richard Weiss, Holt Rinehart and Winston, Inc., 1970;

# Chapter 1

The Black Biblical Heritage by John L. Johnson, Winston Derek Publishers, Inc., 1991; Beyond The Rivers Of Ethiopia by Mensa Otabil, Pneuma Life, 1993. End Sidebar.

First, let's start by examining "basic beliefs." Because I am most familiar with the Christian perspective, I have chosen to focus on Christian beliefs. Let's look at how we perceive characters of the Bible. Often God, Jesus and other Biblical characters are depicted as White Europeans. I grew up believing all-powerful beings were White, be they spiritual, physical, evil, or good. But, we all know these Biblical characters can't be White...or do we? But, research indicates that most of the characters of the Bible were born, lived, worked, and played in a region of the world where people were of color. Archaeological evidence that corroborates Biblical history was found on or near the continent of Africa. This should make us pause and ask, what about the origin of all races of people? American history often neglects to examine the origins of all Americans. The dominant American culture is White and Eurocentric, and that has greatly influenced what we know and believe. Realizing this, many Americans are currently trying to gain a better understanding of what makes America the beautiful. At this time, I will only attempt to answer this question concerning our subject matter of Black people.

Most current research shows that Black people probably originated in Egypt. They had great intelligence, wealth, and royal lineage. Artifacts found in Africa suggest that Black people existed 17,000 thousand years before Christ was born. Some anthropologists believe that in the fifteenth century Black people first encountered Europeans. At this time, Black monarchies had already been established. Despite popular beliefs, Black culture and governmental systems were as advanced as European.

## What Is The Current Thinking On How Blacks Became Americans?

Black people were the first people to discover iron. Unfortunately for them, they did not use iron to build weapons. This was a serious mistake that left Africans vulnerable. In the 15$^{th}$ century, Christopher Columbus discovered America. He recognized the potential of this discovery and the need for labor to develop it. Africa became the source of this labor. In a sense, it was European economic growth that brought Black slaves to America.

Lacking geographic defenses made Africa easy to invade. Lacking metal weaponry made her people easy to subjugate. Africa's proximity to Europe made the temptation irresistible. Africa became a source for much-needed labor. Hence, the Black slave trade was born. Slavery evolved from European trading along the coast of Africa to European land annexation to armed invasion called "pacification." Black slave labor was a vital part of the southern American economy until the mid-nineteenth century when agricultural machinery was developed that could harvest and process produce at a lower cost. (Note: Africans enslaved each other, as one tribe conquered another. I don't know, but doubt, that this slavery was the same as slavery in America, but it may be fair to note that Europeans sometimes bought existing slaves.)

Sidebar – Note: Kareem Abdul-Jabbar and Alan Steinberg recently published a book called Black Profiles In Courage, William and Morrow, 1996. In this book they present the story of a Black man named Estevanico who was the first Black person mentioned by name in American history. According to Jabbar and Steinberg, he was the only Black in the first exploration to cross the North American Continent. Estevanico was not only an explorer; he was one of the first pioneers in America. What is most significant, as these authors so judiciously pointed out, is that he was pre-Columbus. This put Blacks in America before Europeans. Interesting food for thought. End Sidebar.

I believe that this lack of iron weapons resulted in racial prejudice. The African people had no need - and were not prepared - to conquer other peoples, making them easy to conquer. The conquerors considered them weak, both an obstacle blocking their economic progress and a resource to their gaining economic progress. So, the conquerors exploited both the African people and their land. They began to look down on the Africans who were so easily conquered. With this attitude, they focused on the differences between themselves and those they conquered. This is more than enough to build ethnic and racial prejudice. In this frame of mind, they didn't look for the good or the richness of the Africans, but how they could be used to further economic progress through domination. They became convinced that these differences were based on inferiority and primitive mentality. The conquered people can be treated like animals, dehumanized, reduced to beasts of burden. These "inferior beings" were used to accomplish the conquerors objective of building a "brave new world."

As the conquerors became convinced that the Black slave was simply an inferior being to be used for work, they had to continue to override any rational thoughts that might suggest this was wrong. Human nature is probably the hardest foe to conquer with in the thinking process and it often points out your own weaknesses, especially when you really need to be strong.

Recorded history tells us, Blacks arrived in America in the year of 1619. Not until the 1640's is there any evidence that Africans were being consigned to perpetual servitude, and even that evidence is weak. We are fairly certain that, by the 1660's, hereditary slavery was prominent in the colonies. In the eighteenth century, Blacks in most colonies were stripped of virtually all the rights accorded to White settlers under the common law. In many colonies, a Black was not defined as a legal person, but as chattel property. Blacks were discussed as the object of rights, but not as having any rights. Blacks had no rights to religion, marriage, or parenthood. Blacks could not own or carry arms. They could not buy or sell commodities, or engage in any economic activity. Education was forbidden to slaves in most of the colonies; literacy among slaves was also forbidden. The reason for this ban on slave literacy was because of a fear that permitting Black slaves to read would enable "the germ of freedom might grow in him." No more than two or three slaves were allowed to congregate in a public place.

To give you an idea of how well this indoctrination worked, today you can often hear us Black Americans tease each other. When we find ourselves together and there are more than two or three of us standing around talking, we will say to each other, you know more than two of you people standing together constitute a riot. Often, that is followed by hearty laughter, but, once that laughter has subsided, the group usually disperses.

Gary B. Nash, a historian, compared the American slavery system, which was based on race, to a slavery system of the ancient world, which was not based on race. The South American colonies of Spain and Portugal were less repressive than the closed system of servitude established by the British-North American system.

Sidebar: In trying to set up the basis for helping White Americans understand today's Black Americans, it is very important to understand the real or perceived historical perspective that Black Americans learn and hold as truths in their hearts. We are not looking for a right or wrong answer, but we are looking for explanations of how thought processes evolve. We will take up a discussion for understanding the differences between White and Black American thinking in a later chapter. However, we must offer some rationale for how America got to the condition it is currently in. There are some pervasive attitudes around race on the part of both Black and White Americans that stem directly from what we have learned from history. These attitudes were - and still are -very damaging to the American culture, and are the main issues that led to the writing of this book.

I believe slavery was a planned part of building the American dream. Racism and its by-products were side effects that resulted from a system with race and skin color as main criteria for participant selection. I don't want to lead you to believe this was a well thought-out plan, as we are often led to believe. Slavery exacted a high price for the economic success it provided. We who are now living with that success and its consequences often find ourselves dealing with problems that originated when this system was first established. With hindsight, you might say it was like an experiment gone bad and, if we had it to do all over again, we would do it much differently. Understanding how this system was first built offers us some insights as to what we need to do to get this experiment back under control, especially now that the original specimen (Black People) are now a part of the scientific team. Just remember that we (Americans) now have to live with what was created during those early days of America. We have inherited the assets and the liabilities created by that system. End sidebar.

Slavery was only the beginning of the difficult journey of Black people to become Black Americans. The economic system based on slavery was approximately two hundred and forty years old when America realized it had done something ugly that had to be corrected. The result was the Emancipation Proclamation of 1863. At this time, America took its first steps to formally dismantle the economic system based on slavery. This was a great start. But, it took approximately 90 years for Black Americans to realize that they were not much better off under the emancipation system, as long as they didn't have the same rights as White Americans did. In the 1960's, there were massive protest movements. Black America and White America were finally looking each other in the eye.

Sidebar: It is very important to understand, and I will make this point again and again, White Americans were heavily involved in the success of the demonstrations and the organization of these movements. It was a White man's world, and it took White men to help change it. This is still true today and the incentives to change it are greater today than they were 133 years ago.

Voting rights were given to many Black Americans after the revolution around the 1830's. (It was not until 1965 that legislation was passed to remove many obstacles that kept Black Americans from registering to vote. Today, it is still a major task to get Black Americans to vote. I think we are truly becoming Americans; we are as apathetic as the rest of America about exercising our privilege to vote.) End sidebar.

Not until 1955 did Black Americans take their first real calculated steps toward equal rights by organizing the historic bus boycott in Montgomery, Alabama. (There is a good modern-day movie that stars Whoppie Goldberg and Sissy Spacek on video. The movie is titled, "The Long Walk Home.") The boycott consisted of Black Americans organizing car pools and refusing to ride the bus for twelve long months. The main objective of the boycott was to stop segregated seating. White Americans were surprised to find that Black Americans were not happy riding in the back of the bus. They were also surprised to find that Black Americans had the collective thinking to organize such an effective protest. Most White Americans were appalled at the Black Americans' behavior. The Montgomery Bus Company (owned and controlled by White Americans), thought it could ride out the boycott, and Black Americans would soon tire and return to riding "in the back of the bus." The economic effects of the boycott on the transit system was so effective, they forced the system to settle the dispute with Black Americans.

I was two years old when these boycotts began. I still remember standing behind the screen near the middle of the bus, when there were seats empty in front of the screen. I vividly remember paying the fare and entering the bus through the back door. The boycott did not immediately end this practice in New Orleans. I can remember standing behind the screen well into the sixties. Here is a funny note: I love to ride in the back of the bus, now that I am not forced to do so. I often wonder if my comfort in the back of the bus is due to those early life indoctrination and experiences. This indoctrination was accomplished by being forced *legally* to sitting in the rear of the bus. I have noticed the older I get, the less I want to be near the rear of the bus. I have noticed that the young Black American youth seem to congregate near the rear of public transit cars and buses. Interestingly enough, young White American youth follow them to those seats.

The first Civil Rights Act became law in 1957. The law was not very strong, but it did repeal congressional policy established in the late nineteenth century of not interfering in Civil Rights matters pertaining to Black Americans. In 1965-1967, Black civil rights events in Watts, Chicago, Cleveland and Detroit forced the nation to realize that the northern and western states also had the same racial struggles as the south. In 1968, Lyndon B. Johnson established a commission to look into civil rights disorders throughout the nation. The commission's report issued in the spring of 1968 included this very telling statement:

*"Our nation is moving towards two societies, one Black, one White, both separate but unequal. What White Americans have never fully understood and Black Americans can never forget, is that White society is deeply implicated in the ghetto. Most Americans know little of the racial schism between our White and Black citizens. Few appreciate how central the problem of the Black American has been to our social policy. Fewer still understand that today's problem can be solved only if White Americans comprehend how rigid, social, economic and educational barriers have prevented Black Americans from participating in the mainstream of American life."*

The movement toward equality continued in 1960 when four students from a Black college in Greensboro, North Carolina went into a local store, purchased several items, then sat down at the store's lunch counter and ordered coffee. Of course, they were refused service. They stayed seated until the store closed. This started the era of the "sit-ins." Libraries, beaches, restaurants, hotels, and other public facilities were all targeted for sit-ins. The federal government was sympathetic to the movement, and the

Attorney General's Office used its power to negotiate with national chain stores to stop the segregation of lunch counters and other facilities. I remember as a boy of ten or eleven sitting in Woolworth's with my mother at a counter marked "for colored's only." Going to the Avalon theatre in Algiers, a poor, Black suburb of New Orleans, and having to sit in the balcony. I always wondered why White Americans chose to sit at the bottom, since it was harder to see from that vantage point. (It is good to be able to joke about it today. Giggle! Laugh!)

# Chapter
# 2

## Chapter Two - What Is The Modern Day History of Black Americans?

*M*odern day history for most of us started when we were old enough to realize our experiences will affect what we think, say, and do the rest of our lives. For me that started when I was about twelve. This perspective is easier to relate if I stick to the opportunities that were afforded me during that time period. Those opportunities being education and access to the social and economic systems of our wonderful country. I believe tremendous progress has been made throughout my lifetime to enhance relationships between Black and White Americans. However, we have a ton of work yet to do. But, first, let's paint the background of what the world was like then.

The Seventies were exciting times for Black Americans. Because of the Civil Rights Movement, many Black Americans had the chance to attend White colleges. Affirmative Action Programs helped Black Americans to squeeze through corporate doors and peek at the corporate bullpens. Equal Opportunity quotas gave Black Americans a shot at sitting next to their White American counterparts in thriving, yet restricted, office environments. Black Americans learned to network, but realized that this also threatened management, who suspected plans to overthrow or thwart their systems. Black Americans tried to buck "the system" and found it fully intact "not to be bucked by no one." Set-Aside Programs allowed Black Americans to take chances by hanging out their own shingles! A few Black Americans were "quick studies" and, before the system could figure it out, had slipped into a few executive chairs.

In the Eighties, Black Americans made a few dollars and began to have some fun, the country experienced a positive economic turnaround and yet, setbacks in affirmative action programs. Drugs and crimes had taken their toll on the Black American Community. Black Americans began to empower themselves by learning the rules of economics. We stepped into the main tent of the political arena. Jesse Jackson and company (the Rainbow Coalition) took one giant step forward. A plethora of Black Americans became mayors and other high ranking public officials in key municipalities and one was elected a governor. Black Americans looked back and saw, for the first time, how far we had come and how far we still had to go to achieve parity and equity.

The big step backwards for Black Americans happened in the 90's, just when Black Americans felt they were about to get a piece of the action. A number of factors contributed to the progress we made. The Vietnam-era baby boomers started to manage corporate America, and although they are a conservative brood, they are sensible and rational if for no other reason than to make money. The representatives of various European cultures (British, Italians, Germans, Irish and others) who helped shape America's successful industrial age are no longer struggling for their share of American wealth. As a result of an increase in wealth and stature in the business community, White Americans felt more confident than in the 80's. They are the owners of the large corporations. Due to the competitive nature of world commerce and a change in the make-up of the available workforce, this country is going to have to turn back to the ones who helped those Europeans build America, the Black American. Those who also sweat and bled to make America the beautiful. When corporate America started to plan for the workforce of the future, "Workforce for the year 2000," Black Americans figured heavily into the equation. America can't continue to ignore this valuable resource.

As Black Americans acquire more professional skills and interact more with White Americans, our longing to share more of the prosperity and influence of White America increases. We acknowledge our achievements by noting that the system is starting to work and it is finally asking all Americans to take their rightful places. Success is eminent! Affluent is a word most Black Americans have recently learned to pronounce. We have smelled this aroma of success, and we like the fragrance. We now have educated Blacks in every part of this country's economic structure, including corporate America. Yet, we have not had the opportunity to control many commercial enterprises. Black resources are reaching critical mass and finally getting to a point of demanding to be utilized. This is what America always wanted for its people – to have all its people participate in success. In the Nineties, Blacks finally realized, at least in part, The Dream that was so vividly presented to America by Dr. Martin Luther King, Jr. Against the backdrop of these achievements, Affirmative Action was severely attacked. The number of Black college graduates available to enter corporate America is declining, due to affirmative action being repealed by the Supreme Court. Black attendance at colleges has dropped by 80% since those ruling came down. True cause and affect, would you agree?

**"You know, history is a wonderful place to come from, but is often a terrible place to live. Black Americans have been trapped living in history and would love to move away, given the opportunity presents itself."**

### *Who Are Some Of The Important Blacks Who Played Crucial Roles In The Making And Shaping Of America, Yesterday And Today?*

Most of us Americans are poorly informed about the role Black Americans have played in America's past and present. The following Black Americans were instrumental in making America the great country it is today. (Most of this information was taken from the Black Heritage Day Book II written and researched by Carl Bernard Mack, 1995.)

**Dr. Alexa Canady** - Born 1950 - At the age of thirty, she became the first Black American woman to become a neurosurgeon in the history of the United States. The American Board of Neurological Surgery certified her in 1984. She continues to teach in major medical institutions around the country.

**Reverend Jesse Jackson** - Born 1941 – He started his Civil Rights Activist career by joining the Southern Christian Leadership Conference (SCLC) when Dr. Martin Luther King Jr. was the SCLC president. He became a close confidant of Dr. King, and was with him when he was assassinated. He was the founder of Operation PUSH (People United to Save Humanity) and the Rainbow Coalition, which is still responsible for organizing efforts that lead to positive, political, social, and economic changes in America. Reverend Jackson was the first Black American man to make a serious bid for the United States Presidency. His bid was so strong that it erased the notion that a Black American could never be elected President. As a result of his encouragement, more Black Americans registered to vote than ever before in the history of the United States. Rev. Jackson continues to negotiate fair business and employment practices for Black Americans with major corporate entities.

**General Colin Powell** - Born 1938 – He was both the first Black American and the youngest man to attain the office of the Chairman of the Joint Chiefs of Staff. He was the first Black American to serve as the national security advisor to the President of the United States. Gen. Powell was also the first Black American to be wooed by the Republican Party to run for President of the United States.

**Dr. Martin Luther King, Jr.** – 1929-1968 – He became the youngest recipient of the Nobel Peace Prize for his work in organizing and orchestrating non-violent activities that included:

- Boycott of city buses in Montgomery, Alabama
- Protest of unfair hiring practices in Birmingham, Alabama
- Voter Registration in Selma, Alabama
- Open housing and slum rehabilitations in Chicago, Illinois
- Opposition to the Vietnam War

Dr. King is the only Black American to be honored with a national holiday. It is still not observed throughout all of America.

**Shirley Chisolm** - Born 1924 – She was the first Black American woman to be elected to the United States House of Representatives. In 1972 she was the first Black American woman to make a bid for the presidential nomination of the Democratic Party, for which she received 150 of 1600 delegates.

**Thurgood Marshall** – 1908-1993 - In 1954 he argued the most pivotal case in American public education, Brown vs. Board of Education. As the head of the NAACP Legal Defense Fund, he convinced the Supreme Court to rule "separate but equal" school systems as unconstitutional. He was the first Black American appointed to the highest court in the land, the United States Supreme Court.

**Dr. Charles Drew** - 1904 -1950 – He revolutionized medical treatment when he discovered a process to separate and preserve blood, resulting in blood plasma. In 1940 he was recognized for his expertise in blood plasma. The British government requested his leadership in setting up the first blood bank in England. He was appointed the director of the American Red Cross during World War II. Later, he resigned when the War Department insisted that blood from White American donors be kept separate from that of Black American donors. He also served as Professor of Surgery at Howard Medical School.

**George Washington Carver** - 1864-1943 – His extensive research with peanut and soybeans led to the development of more than 300 by-products from the peanut, including milk, butter, paper, and face cream, ink, and dyes. Although he only patented three of his discoveries, these patents cover several processes for manufacturing paints and stains from clay and minerals.

For an exciting study of many more Black Americans who made and continue to make significant contributions to building America, read Black Heritage Day II, 1995 written by Carl Bernard Mack.

### *What Are Some Of The Facts About Black Americans?*

This section is very important and will help you better understand more about the Black Americans that live, work and play with you. This information is not meant to be comprehensive or to overwhelm you with numbers or statistics, but to provide you with information that will help you understand your fellow Black Americans as a people. I am impressed when someone takes the time to learn about my background and about who I am as an individual. Most Blacks will be impressed if you know something about them as a people and as individuals. I can't help you with the individual part, that you should have fun doing on your own. I encourage you, after learning as much as you wish about us as a people, to work hard at getting to know Black people on an individual basis and personal level. You should be pleasantly surprised to find they are neat people, just like you.

Many Americans want to know more about each other, but due to our busy schedules, don't take time to research things that could help us in our relationships with one another. I am guilty of this, too. Many people make assumptions about each other based on outdated information – worse, they make decisions using this outdated information. The way we think about each other is often born out of the information we have and, if that information is outdated, so is our thinking.

The information presented in this section is a snap shot in time of some of the statistics that come from the news media and other sources. I wanted most of it to come from the media because that is what most of us Americans rely on as our source of information. If you are reading this book ten years or more after it was written, the data will be dated. In this case, you should compare this data to data that currently exists.

### How Many Black Americans Are There In The Good Old USA Today?

I would like to approach this question with an overview of the whole world. (Data source: Dr. John Taborn, University of Minneapolis, 1995). If you took a representative sample of 100 people out of the world: 21 of them would be White (of European descent), 57 of them would be Asians, 14 of them would be from North and South America, and only 8 of them would be Black (of African descent).

If we looked at the 1990 United States Census data, we would find the following:

Black of African descent: approximately **30 million, 12.3%** of the American population (10 year growth rate 13.2%) as compared to

• White of European descent: approximately **199.7 million, 83.9 %** of the American population (10 year growth rate 6.0%).
(Data source: 1990 Census Data.)

### How Are The Black Children Faring In America?

**In 1988**

• **63.7 %** of Black American children were born out of wedlock.

• **68 %** of Black American girls become pregnant by the age of 18.

---

- **44%** of Black American children live below the poverty line.
- **50%** drop-out rates are reported by urban schools (Some data show rates approaching 66% percent.)
- **56%** of all Black American households are headed by women — **56%** of these households had incomes below the poverty level.

(Data source: The State of Black America, National Urban League, 1993.)

Interesting correlations to consider are:

The percentage of Black children finishing high school corresponds to the percentage of teenage pregnancies. The percentage of households headed by women correlates with the percentage of Black families at the poverty level.

## How Many Black Men Are Tied Up In the Criminal Justice System?

Young Black American men have a tough time in this country. The following statistics might help you understand how they are faring. Of the young Black men between the ages of 20 and 29 in state and federal prisons:

**32%** of young Black American men are incarcerated.

**7%** of young White American men are incarcerated.

(Data source: The Sentencing Project, 1996)

## What About Black Americans And Drug Usage?

Many Black Americans are involved with the true "Black Plague," drugs. Drugs have been devastating to Black American communities. There is a high correlation between Black youths involved with drugs and Black youths who are incarcerated:

**13%** of all young Black Americans are monthly drug users.

Note: The paper presenting this data did not have the statistics for White Americans.

(Data source: The Sentencing Project, 1996.)

## How Educated Are Black Americans?

The following data measures education levels for ages 15 years and older.

· Nearly **11.5%** of Black Americans are college educated, as compared to **25.2%** of White Americans.

· In 1989 Black Americans earned **5.7%** of all bachelor degrees.

(Data source: Bureau of Census, Education Attainment in the U.S. 1990 and 1991.)

This suggests that educational opportunities are not equally available for Black Americans as for White Americans.

## How Employed Are Black Americans?

- **12.4%** of Black Americans are unemployed
- **6%** of White Americans are unemployed
- **6.7%** of all races combined are unemployed.

(Data source: Prepares National Urban League from unpublished Bureau of Labor and Statistics data, 1993.)

These statistics indicate an inequity in the employment opportunities in America.

## What Is The Life Expectancy Of Black Americans?

- Infant mortality rate for Black American babies is **18.6%** as compared to **8.1%** for White American babies.
- Black American women are expected to live **74.3** years as compared to **79.7** years for White American women.
- Black American men are expected to live **65.6** years as compared to **73.0** years for White American men.

(Data Source: U.S. Department of Health and Human Services, 1991.)

What might be the reason for these differences? The availability of health care must figure into the picture, and the availability of health care is affected by social-economic status.

**What Is The Income Level Of Black Americans?**

• The median income for Black Americans is $21,548 as compared to $37,783 for White Americans.

• Buying power for Black Americans on an annual base is approaching $400 Billion.

(Bureau of the Census, Money Income of Households, Families and Persons in the U.S., 1991.)

These statistics clearly show an inequity of opportunity for Black Americans. There are many reasons for these inequities. I hope you might research this further to gain a better understanding of the significance of these statistics.

Hopefully, this chapter gives you a new perspective on the history and condition of Black America. More than that, I hope it peaked your curiosity to make you want to learn more about fellow Americans. Most important of all, make sure you come to your own conclusions about Black Americans as a people and as individuals.

# Chapter
# 3

## Chapter Three - Is Black American Thinking Different From White American Thinking?

*T*he question is not, do Blacks and Whites think differently, because the answer to that question is an unequivocal Yes! No! Sometimes! And most certainly! If the question was phrased, do Blacks think differently from their White counterparts based on the life they experience in America? Then the answer to this question is the main subject matter of this chapter.

Sidebar - Digression: In America the goals are to become as much like each other as we possibly can. However, the American assimilation process does not allow this to come to what one might be led to believe is the final natural conclusion. Yes, there are times when we should fight what assimilation attempts to do to the American culture, especially when it adversely affects an American sub-cultural or ethnic group. American culture has lost much of the richness of the German, Italian, Swedish, Irish, Norwegian and all those other neat, rich ethnic cultures that make up the European heritage. The assimilation process slowly wipes them out. Each ethnic sub-culture has its own thinking process. For better or worse, these processes have been lost. I will delve into the assimilation process quite heavily in the next chapter. End Sidebar

We all think distinctively—no matter what color, race or ethnicity we are, as a result of our life experiences —based on life experiences, based on the color of your skin in America, which leads to a certain set of experiences in America. But the question on the table is, do Black and White Americans as groups think differently? This question can't be answered with an emphatic one-word answer, either. Let's ask this question in a different form. Is Black American thinking different than White American thinking? It depends on what you ask us to think about. The same is true for White Americans. If you ask the average White American do you need food to sustain the body? She will give you an emphatic yes! If you ask the average Black American do you need food to sustain the body. She will give you an emphatic yes. If you go deeper into that question and ask the question, what kinds of food do you need to sustain the body? The average White American might say vegetables, steak, fish, whole grain bread, pasta, and diet soda. The average Black American might say beans, chicken, catfish, cornbread, rice, and Barq's Root Beer. Are there different thought processes applied here? You bet! The difference lies in the experiences these two average Americans have had. They both gave you the same food groups, but their life experiences lead to different types of food in the same food groups. To this day, I think diet soda is not the real thing. I grew up on good OLE sweet Coca-Cola, Pepsi cola, and root beer. Even as I write this paragraph, I am drinking a coke in the red can (with sugar).

Most of the people who are sitting on the plane with me as I am typing this paragraph are White. I asked the flight attendant whether they serve more diet or straight coke? He said, diet. I am not going to give you a lot of empirical data to clutter your mind, but I do want to give you some concrete examples that may help you understand that there are differences.

### *How Important Is It To Understand The Differences In How White And Black Americans Think?*

The essences of our problems in America are centered around race. If people are thinking about each other in a way that is not healthy and or productive, their relationships will be destroyed. As long as I think you don't like me, I will not want to make any conciliatory steps toward you. I will do everything in my power to prepare myself to deal with you and to minimize the harm you can do to me. I have found many of my White colleagues and friends are afraid of my Black colleagues and friends. Some of what these White people think is so bizarre

Black America also has paranoid thoughts about White America. Too often we Blacks will bring to reality what never existed before they became fully conceived thoughts. For example, I was working on a project with one of my White colleagues who was trying to understand what one of my Black colleagues wanted from a partnership that I and some of my cohorts put together. Now get this! My Black colleague owns a business that employs several White engineers. My White colleague, who was responsible for the overall management of the project, decided that all my Black colleague wanted was to make as much money as he could and that he didn't care about the other players working on the project. My White colleague told me that my Black colleague was taking advantage of us and he wanted to do something about the situation. It turned out that my Black colleague's decisions were being negotiated by one of his White engineers. The two White engineers were not able to come to agreement! I quickly analyzed the situation, and had both parties work through me. Later, I heard my White colleague repeat that my Black colleague's team was just trying to get what they could out of the project. The real issue was no one wanted to relinquish control to the other. I came up with a quick solution to the project that led to a win-win. They (my Black colleague and his White engineer employee) would simply do their part of the work according to the standards and terms we had previously documented and agreed to. The main term was the price for the work done. My White colleague and I would not dictate how the work was to be done and we would not support them in any way except to review the work and decide if it met our standards. The impasse was over. The interesting part about this event was that my colleagues were so caught up in the way they thought about each other, they had not taken the time to think with each other. The White engineer who worked for my

Black colleague admitted, he simply did not want to be controlled by my White colleague. He had assimilated into this Black-owned Company and its way of thinking. Black Americans work hard not to be controlled by White Americans. Interesting, wouldn't you say?

### *Are White Supremacy Thought Patterns Embedded In America?*

If you ask a White American would they want to be Black in America, almost all of them would tell you an emphatic, "NO WAY!" It is not that they think there is no hope for Black people, they have simply observed Black American life and have decided it is not the "Best Life" in America. Are you right for thinking that way? Yes! You remember the scene in "Star Wars," when Ben Kenobe told Luke Skywalker, his father was dead. In a later scene, Yoda revealed to Luke, his father was Darth Vader. Luke then turned to Obi-Wan and said, "You lied to me, you told me my father was dead." Ben said, "I didn't lie to you. I answered you from a certain point of view." You see, in Ben's eyes, Anakin Skywalker, Luke and Lea's father, died when the dark side of the force seduced him. Whites see Blacks from a certain point of view, a White one. From that point of view, a Black American does not have as good a life as a White American. For example, many White Americans consider themselves better than Black Americans, even if there are some Black Americans who have achieved a higher level of financial success than some White Americans. In America, success is not defined as the amount of money a person has, but the amount of opportunity that is available to you.

White Americans can quickly assess the situation for Black and White Americans and determine that Black Americans have far fewer opportunities. Woven into the fabric of American culture is the assumption that Blacks have fewer opportunities than Whites! Have Whites developed a set of false assumptions? Maybe! If so, these assumptions have been embedded over time into the American culture. Even Black's think that they shouldn't do as well as Whites. As a person who has attained some of the finer things in life, I catch myself thinking that I have somehow risen above being Black. Instead, I should realize that I live in America, the land of opportunity. While opportunities are not necessarily equitable, there are numerous opportunities for Blacks in America. Our problem lies in our accepting class-based assumptions about Blacks and Whites.

Consider this scenario. You are walking on the top floor of one of the bank tower buildings in a city anywhere in America. The sign over the door says SENIOR VICE PRESIDENT OF OPERATIONS. You look in the office and you see a Black guy sitting in a chair looking out over the city. He has no tie on, but is dressed nicely. Be honest and tell me your first thought. Is he the Sr. Vice President of Operations, or is he some maintenance guy playing executive by sitting in an office with a view? Interestingly, you probably guessed correctly. It is unlikely that a Black man will have a powerful position in a bank. By the way, in this example the Black Guy was the VP of Operations and had just stopped in his office to pick up some papers to work on while he flies to some small town to look at expanding operations of the bank. Consider the same example from a Black perspective: "Hmmm! That brother must have worked very hard to be sitting in that office. I wonder how old he is and how much money he makes. He doesn't even have to wear a tie! How did he get so high up?"

Now, modify the scenario so that the guy in the chair is White with a three-day-old beard, in sweats, and uncombed hair. A White observer may think the VP must live in the city, just finished running, and decided he needed to return to the office to finish some work. The Black observer probably thinks the same as the White observer: "Man, white folks can do whatever they want when they reach the top." In reality, in this example, the White man was the nephew of the CEO and was only playing executive. Black and White Americans clearly think differently, based on our different experiences.

There are many Black Americans who think being Black in America is not a good thing. Some of the experiences have influenced them to think this way. But, Black Americans love America. They may not be pleased with how America treats them or what America may think about them, but they love America. The biggest problem we face in Black thought is our ability to constantly try to reconcile why things are the way they are. The problem is cognitive dissonance. We must force our thinking to line up with reality. This is what every human being lives to do. Things truly are the way I think they are. Hmmm!

I love being a Black in America and, therefore, being a Black American. I do not think there is a better country to live in on the face of the earth. I have had the opportunity to visit other foreign countries. The strongest urge I have when the plane lands on the West Coast of America is to kiss the ground, just like every other red-blooded American. Is it always easy to express this love for America? No! Not when America is represented by the KKK, the Aryan Nation, the Black Panther Party, the Crips, and the Bloods. But, when all is said and done, I love being an American and you can quote me. However, I often find my thoughts don't line up with what is in front of me. I often realize I'm comparing myself to others. This only causes me problems when I realize I am not trying to be the best person I can be, but the best Black person I can be. You don't understand yet do you? Let me try to make it clearer.

I am successful by American standards. I own a home in Beaverton, Oregon that at the time of authoring this book was appraised for tax purposes at $326,000 dollars. Every time I turn my blue Jaguar into the Heceta cul-de-sac, I feel I am out of place. Yes, I am the only Black man living in the Burntwood neighborhood, a highly affluent suburb. My wife is Filipino and my children are, well you can figure that out. My neighbors are all wonderful people and I can't sense any prejudice from our interactions. Most of them are typical nice, hardworking upper middle class White Americans. But, my own upbringing in Southern America taught me that Blacks live in the poorest part of town, and Whites live everywhere else. I know that this has changed over the last twenty years, but my experience has resulted in a frame of mind that is me at odds with my own reality. When I was a child, we weren't allowed to be in a White neighborhood at night, unless we were working for someone who live there. As I shared earlier, when I was ten in New Orleans, I had to ride behind the screen on the public transit system. Blacks were not allowed to ride in front of the screen – that was reserved for White people. I am not giving you this information to make you, as White Americans, feel sorry for Black Americans. I am telling you this so you will be able to understand how and why Black Americans think the way we do.

### *What Do Black Americans Think About White Americans?*

Most Blacks think that White Americans only care about themselves. Whites are very exclusive and, if they had their way, they would just put us back on the boat and send us somewhere far from America. A particular feature of the television news program "20/20" focused on Blacks opinions about Whites. I was shocked at some of the discussion I heard. There was Black people who felt that the White government is creating ways to get rid of Blacks. There were Blacks who felt that certain companies make products to actually hurt them. One product they thought was developed to hurt Blacks and not Whites is "Snapple." I absolutely love "Snapple," and drink a lot of it. It was scary to hear that a large number of Blacks think Snapple is an anti-Black drink. They tout the markings on the bottle as being subliminal messages that are anti-Black. The truth of the matter is they mistook the picture on the label that represents the Boston Tea Party as a Black slavery ship. Could they be right? You can see how careful we must be in presenting our history.

I have heard many of my Black friends say that AIDS is a disease that was deliberately established in America to get rid of Black people. How much more destructive can our thinking get? I do not believe that AIDS is an agent for the genocide of Black Americans! We who truly care about America and want it to continue to be the land of the free and the brave must put measures in place to help extinguish this kind of thinking. And, if some of you White folks were foolish enough to dream up a scheme such as this, shame on you. (Just joking! Yea, I know, bad joke. I do not believe that.) This type of thinking can be destructive to American society. If we continue not to reach a healthier understanding about each other and this type of paranoid thinking grows more pervasive, we will face a serious enemy that will be in our midst. It will be us! Most of us know that AIDS will kill any human it can, without regard to race. Even the rich can't slow the effects of AIDS, because you can't buy more time like you can with diseases that are prevented with better healthcare or better healthcare providers.

It would be easy for Whites to say that this is ludicrous thinking, but fear is a powerful force and, if you add a lack of knowledge and positive experiences, you can easily slip into paranoid thinking. This type of thinking is a ticking time bomb in America. It led to the riots in Los Angeles when the Rodney King verdict was handed down. People only need a little bit of spark to ignite fear-laden thoughts that the majority of the population does not want you among them.

Some young White teenage men share similar line of thoughts that, as a result of fear and a lack of education, their rights and privileges are being eroded by Affirmative Action and other social programs. The situation is worsened when they are fed propaganda by people who live to make hate a tool of division among American Blacks and Whites. Case in point: I was once asked to consult at an alternative high school that had some White supremacy activity. I gladly accepted the work, because I love sharing knowledge with teenagers. I found these kids to be ordinary, regular, everyday teenagers with two exceptions. Now get this! These kids had been segregated from their peers and friends due to some policy the regular school system put in place to correct truancy. These kids also had very little experience with people who were different from them. Add to this, the kids had received information that not only was fraught with stupidity, but also grossly inaccurate.

The first thing I found out about these kids was that they were starving for information. I presented them with demographic data about their area. They argued with me that my data was wrong. They thought the Black population was growing at a tremendous rate and Blacks out numbered them greatly. In the part of the country where they live, Blacks only represent 1.6% of the state population. Most of them had never spent any time with Black people. They mainly knew Blacks from television. I finally convinced them that my data came from the government census and was the best data available even with its margin for error. They immediately paid close attention to the rest of my presentation. They never stopped questioning my statistics, and I encouraged the debate. I asked questions like, what should we do with all the Black people in the United States? They said they didn't know. I suggested sending them back to Africa, reminding them of how much money it would cost them, using the government to accomplish this gigantic task. They laughed right along with me at how stupid that suggestion sounded. We continued brainstorming, and the kids and I laugh at the ideas. I spent two hours with them, and was amazed how brainwashed they were by some backward-thinking grown-ups.

I had a fun time working with these kids. I went to lunch with them and we talked about sports, politics and many other subjects normal thinking teenagers care to discuss and comprehend. I asked them, if you all hate Blacks so much, why are you letting me into the circle. They simply replied, you are okay. I would like to tell you that I solved all the problems of this little school, but the truth is, I didn't. The next week they had more white supremacist graffiti on one of the chairs. White supremacy had become a part of their thinking, and it takes a lot more than a hotshot consultant like me to waltz in and change their thinking. They had a belief system that was being fed by some bad people, in my opinion. When I worked with their teachers, I sensed some support for supremacy beliefs. This even scared me.

Blacks think Whites have it made in America. When all the models for success are White, what else can you expect? All across America our success models are White, with the exception of cities like Atlanta, D.C., or Chicago. But, even when I visit those cities, the poorest Americans are still Black Americans. I hate to visit the south side of Chicago because it is so depressing. I only go there because the best restaurant in town is on the south side of Chicago.

The media, which I shall discuss later, continues to present Whites very positive in all aspects of life. Television commercials show Whites brushing their teeth; seldom do commercials show Blacks using Aqua Fresh or Scope. If you let the media be your teacher, most of our criminals appear to be Black.

Every fortune 500 company has Whites in most of the top positions. The majority of the bankers are White. Banks are trying to change this, and are having some success. On the other hand, I give the fast food industry credit for making their workforce look more like their customers. McDonalds, Burger King and Wendy's all reach out to hire young Black youth. Most of the bus drivers I see across America are black. Sports have a lot of Black Americans and I shall discuss them in a later chapter.

Black American thought patterns and attitudes have developed over two hundred years, based on many negative experiences and beliefs. It will take time to change. I don't think it will take another two hundred years, but it will take more time than we think it will. We must first understand what needs to be fixed, and put the processes in place to get them fix.

## *What Do Black Americans Think White Americans Think About Them?*

Most Blacks think that White Americans would rather not think about them. Many Blacks think that Whites sit around and plot how they are going to eradicate the Black population in America. This is very volatile thinking and, as I have said above, it leads to riots, and generally acts as a catalyst for violence in America. I see the Hispanic population starting to think similarly. This even scares an optimist like me. Many events in the world continue to foster this dangerous line of thinking.

While I was writing this section, a disenchanted, downsized employee tape-recorded the Texaco Company's top management. They were discussing Black workers in a very demeaning fashion. Texaco's stock fell over a billion dollars in one week. I remember examining my personal feelings while viewing the CEO on "Nightline." Ted Koppel, Nightline's spokesman, asked the CEO why Black employees of Texaco should believe him when he says he will not tolerate discriminatory behavior, since he hadn't done anything to stop that behavior so far. As the CEO attempted to explain his position, I thought, he was trying to save his butt and his job. Totally slipping into a Black frame of mind, I realized I hadn't tried to tell if he was being sincere. I was ashamed of my own prejudgment. I believe he was ready to do whatever necessary to rectify the ugly situation, regardless of his motivation or incentives. I grew up near a Texaco station that was one of the main parts of our community. I now think Texaco is a place where Black Americans are treated poorly. Texaco will never be able to stop Blacks from thinking they are out to get rid of them after this type of behavior by its senior management staff. They are in the midst of the "usual" court settlement in an attempt to buy back the loyalty of their workers.

Sidebar: A short digression: These types of incidents affect White employees as much as the Black employees. Texaco's employee morale will plummet for many months until Texaco can demonstrate that it has truly changed its philosophy and implemented a new policy, that is, demonstrate it has changed its corporate culture and thinking. White and Black employees will not trust each other. The tensions between Black and White co-workers will grow to disruptive levels, and the corporate profits will suffer for at least a year. The Denny Restaurants Corporation could attest to the impact of a single negative racial event. The good news is Denny's successfully worked for three years to correct the situation. I am eating at Denny's again. Denny's new CEO has gone on record stating the company has changed and will never be the same again. Denny's stock values are back on top and they are selling more food to Black and White America than ever before. End Sidebar.

As I am writing this book, California passed a measure (Measure 209) that will eliminate Affirmative Action. When the measure passed, most Black Americans believed this meant the country really does not care about us. The Whites and Blacks who voted for this measure truly believed they were doing the right thing. The measure in essence said, vote yes to stop discrimination. Now who in their right mind would vote no? Most Black Americans knew this measure was to turn back time. They thought Whites passed this measure so they could stop providing opportunities for Black Americans. These types of events build walls between White and Black Americans. I believe if White Americans truly understood the progress we Blacks made due to Affirmative Action, they would not have voted to abolish it. Regardless of whether the measure was right or wrong, the message the Black community heard was clearly divisive. We must become smarter in seeing the results of ballot measures, judging them by their effect and not by any possible good intentions their authors had.

## Chapter 3

### *How Do Black Americans Really Think?*

This is a question that should be answered by every Black American for every White American that asks! Black Americans, in a nutshell, are chameleon-like thinkers. Our thoughts vary according to the surroundings we are in. When you have been placed in as many different and death-defying situations as Blacks have in America, you must become a chameleon in order to survive. We can change our spots or colors when we are given time to understand our surroundings. Our thinking is very adaptable and flexible and, some times, too tolerable. Our skin on the other hand is indelible, and we wouldn't want it any other way.

I've classified Black thought into different groups based on experience, social climate, economic climate, political climate and how we perceive America is progressing. This is not a comprehensive list. I know I run the risk of perpetuating some stereotypes of Black Americans, but I think it is very import to provide you with some insights as to how Black Americans think and what influences our thoughts.

### Ghetto Thinking

On the lowest social economic rung of the ladder stands the ghetto dweller. I was one of for many years. The ghetto experience is analogous to alcoholism. Neither the ghetto-dweller nor the alcoholic is ever free from past experiences or the effects.

The thinking in the ghetto is one of ultimate survival. I grew up in the ghetto of Algiers, a predominantly Black urban suburb of New Orleans, Louisiana (That's "New- Or-Leans," not "Norlans" as a lot of northerners have learned from Cajun commercialism.), in the Fisher Housing Project. I have experienced life first-hand in the ghetto. It is not just a physical state of being, it is also a state of mind. The ghetto is truly a neighborhood, or, as we have nicknamed it, the "Hood." It is a place inhabited by the Black American Poor. It can be dangerous, but often, unbeknownst to most people, a place of comfort and joy. Many ghetto dwellers have not experienced other ways of living, so they don't often know how bad it is compared to other types of American life. They mainly live on resources provided by the government or the streets – drugs, theft, and other criminal activities. But, there are many ghetto dwellers who have complete family units and experience financially poor, yet happy, lives. Even the "happy" ghetto dwellers don't have many inspired or hopeful thoughts. Because of this mindset, in the 50's and 60's there was a lot of unrest and turmoil in American communities. However, this mindset was very necessary to help White America see how desperate Black Americans were for improvements in their living conditions. Dr. Martin Luther King, Jr. harnessed this thinking, redirecting it to focus on and bring about the Civil Rights movement.

Most ghetto dwellers learn to hold tight to the few resources they have. I believe this is why – to this day – I hate to throw away food still on my plate when I am full. Ghetto-dwellers tend to believe they will not have what they need tomorrow, because they barely had enough for today. I don't remember not having food, but I do remember not having a variety or large quantities of food. I hated red beans and rice for years after I left New Orleans, because we had them with fried chicken on many Sundays – that was considered the poor Black American Sunday dinner. The beans were cheap and a pound served a family of four for two days. I was well into my 30's before I started eating them again. Today it is hilarious to watch my White church friends rush to my house, when they know we are going to have red beans and rice.

The ghetto teaches low self-esteem and distrust. Negative activities, thoughts, and a non-supportive environment bombard them. There is little education in the ghetto. Anyone who gets an education leaves the ghetto for a better life, and that is the way it should be. This constantly shapes the way kids think, always focusing on how to get out of the ghetto. When I finished high school, I used the military as my escape. I never returned to the ghetto, except to visit it and notice how much worse it has become – and it has become much, much worse.

Chapter 3

In the ghetto, White Americans are hated and are blamed for all the problems in the ghetto. This is a bit unfair to the White Americans of today, but we all inherit "the sins of our fathers," whether we like it or not. Most of the time, the only White Americans in the ghetto are the police or other governmental authorities. Because of this, many Black Americans think poorly of White Americans, especially those who end up living under those conditions. With a limited exposure to White Americans, ghetto-dwellers have become very angry with White Americans. Sometimes allowing that anger become pure hatred. This thinking lacks hope and can be very destructive.

## Lower Middle Class Black American Thinking

Black Americans at this social economic level have probably concluded that there is some hope in the world today, but believe that there is very little hope of their moving upward socially and economically. They quickly resigned themselves to be satisfied with the status quo, because it is not likely to get much better. They are usually consumed with what comes next, and despair is not far away from them. But, they would never admit they have surrendered to their current economic achievement and all hope of improving their economic position.

In general, many Black Americans are angry at society and blame White America for all the things that are not right in the entire world. Like the ghetto dwellers, they mainly experience White Americans as authority figures. They often think they work to serve White America and can only have blue-collar jobs. They go to work to make money and to make ends meet. They think their paycheck is life and death and are usually devastated when they find themselves out of work. They don't own much and don't understand why. They are most likely to be apartment dwellers and live in conditions that are only a little better than the ghetto. They think of themselves as second class citizens (as compared to people who have been deemed the poor White trash of America.)

They think about the future but not very far out. They spend a lot of time trying to figure out a way they can make the world a better place for their children. In New Orleans, where I grew up, the majority of the community is made up of these people. I spent a lot of time going to school with these people; they were my family and friends.

These are also people, given the chance, that will destroy their community to protest when they believe America is not treating them fairly. During the time I was writing this chapter, a Black person was killed in Florida. The press led the community to believe that a White Police officer shot and killed an unarmed Black man who resisted arrest for speeding. The community came unglued and started destroying the neighborhood.

This was also the thinking that was pervasive in Watts (Los Angeles) during the riots set off by the Rodney King verdict. Rodney King represented a large part of that community whose little hope was being taken away by the LAPD officers who brutally beat Rodney King. These are the people who cheered when O. J. was found not guilty. They didn't allow themselves to analyze the case, which they were quite capable of doing. It was simply a matter of the system attempting to tar and feather another Black man. They simply wanted to see a Black man beat the system.

## Middle Class Black American Thinking

This is a fairly new set of Black American thinkers. They think like Middle Class White America, with one big difference: they know they are Black and what that means to White Americans. This knowledge of being Black in America is very powerful. It brings with it fear, some hostilities, and potential for explosive actions. But these thinkers are educated, and they are products of affirmative action. They know that there is hope, and they see it in their future. They are both excited and fearful of what the future may bring. They are not easily deterred from their mission, to make America recognize that they are a part of this country and will not be denied their rights or the resources to participate in success.

As stated above, these thinkers are educated, but they need more knowledge, knowledge gained from experiencing sustained success. They represent the first generation of educated Black thinkers, the generation of educated Black Americans. They know they need to work together to bring about change and social development. They are still learning the power of community and collective thinking. They are learning they need each other in order to overcome some of the barriers to assimilation. They are still learning to identify opportunities, and, when they find them, move quickly into the upper middle class thinkers, which I shall discuss in the next section. I was one of these thinkers for quite a while. I believe my time as one of these thinkers was well spent, and I was able to capitalize on several opportunities due to the time I spent in corporate America.

These thinkers tend to be entrepreneurial in their approach to work. They lack capital, but are learning to become business owners. They still spend too many resources trying to enhance their image and identity. They waste a lot of time trying to convince themselves that they truly are capable of doing what they have already started to do.

One of the things that this group has accomplished is the internalization of the benefits of education. They manage their resources to ensure education for Black American youth.

These thinkers thought O.J. was not guilty. But, they believe that for a Black man to beat the American justice system, he had to use his money. They don't think the system is fair, but continue to hope and to try to change it for all people.

## Upper Middle Class Black American Thinking

I consider myself a part of this privileged group of thinkers. You probably have a good sense of what and how I think by reading the earlier chapters of this book. As a group, they have taken advantaged of affirmative action as an opportunity and are ready for the next set of objectives and challenges. They are very well educated and know how to use their education. We still struggle with how we make education fully pay off outside of White corporate America. Our main weapon to bring about change in the corporate world is entrepreneurship. These people have used the American Corporation to gain a certain amount of wealth and as their training ground for how to conduct business in America.

We are thinking more and more as entrepreneurs, and, as such, are now demanding our place at the table of opportunity. Although we are starting our own businesses, we are still discovering how to incorporate and implement excellence in our products, goods and services. We still struggle to be taken serious by venture capitalists and by those who hold the purse strings of the American banking system, which still systematically discriminates against us. We have learned to invest for the future, but we still don't know how to obtain wealth more quickly. We have very good ideas, but have not yet learned to work as a community (as people living in Africa do) so that we can capitalize on our collective resources. We truly have trouble understanding how to financially capitalize our own businesses. We are making a lot of mistakes, as did White Americans when they first started creating wealth. Black Americans need White Americans to help them learn these all important skills.

We are not afraid of pushing through the assimilation process, but we are still not willing to give up or compromise our identity. We struggle with our history more than any of the other Black thinkers, because we have analyzed the injustices in America during the last three hundred years and understand how this affects us today. We are in the process of finding and implementing solutions to racial enmity.

We are incorporating education into all our plans. We know the value of investing in our kids and their education. Unlike the White Upper Middle Class, we are doing much better than our parents. We are extremely motivated, and the anger we may still feel against America fuels our progress, as opposed to holding us back. Our kids are the first generation to be surprised and appalled that **you** would allow racism to exist in any fashion. They are as educated with as many positive experiences as your children, and view themselves as their equal and as their peers. Our children are very inclusive, and assume they will participate in all aspects of America especially, the education process. They will expect your children to understand the message in this book and more. They will be surprised if your children read this book for any other reason other than to be amused.

These thinkers thought O.J Simpson to be guilty, but continue to hope he is not. They see the O.J. case as a test of how the system treats people with money and how it treats Blacks.


## Upper Class Black American Thinking

These Black American thinkers truly understand how to assimilate into America and maintain their identity, assuming they achieved this status by hard work. A person only gets to this spot by thoroughly understanding American systems and processes. Part of this system is luck, but I personally do not subscribe due to the unpredictability luck demonstrates.

This is a strange set of thinkers. They spend a lot of time overcoming obstacles and moving their own agenda forward. There are not many of these thinkers in America. Bill Cosby, Oprah Winfry, Michael Jackson, Tiger Woods (due to the guidance he is receiving from his father Earl Woods), and Reginald Lewis (the deceased CEO of Beatrice Foods) would fit in this category. I do not include many of the athletes who have made their money through mere physical talent and no education. Michael Jordan would surely fit in this class, but I have not seen any substantial results in the community that he has accomplished with his money. Earvin "Magic" Johnson could possibly fit in this class, given some of his accomplishments in the business world. The average professional Black American athlete belongs in the middle and lower middle class thinking categories, not in this category. Although money alone doesn't qualify someone to be in this classifications, a person must have a lot of money to be included in this group.

These thinkers definitely believe O.J. is guilty, but hope the media will find another story to hype. These thinkers have become an integral part of the American fabric. They exercise control over much of their own socio-economic destiny. White Americans know who they are, and accept them. They often see this small, but elite, group to be the result of a fluke of American success (opportunity?). Although White Americans are glad that these Blacks have been successful, they have no idea how this could happen in the Black Race. (Hmmmm!)

# Chapter
# 4

## Chapter Four - Why Don't Black Americans Fully Assimilate Into America?

One of our biggest struggles in America is to continue to define ourselves as Americans. You see, to be American means to continue defining who you are as part of a life long process. And, Americans are forced to redefine themselves over and over again. You have experienced this in many ways by now. Your family was once Italian, German, Swedish, Danish, Irish or some other ethnicity that makes up European culture and the White race. Today, most White Americans hardly ever think about their ethnic heritage. The latest Europeans to enter this process are the Russians, who are now in the process of defining themselves as Americans. They, too, will be successful, as soon as the first generation of Russian Americans are born and educated in America. Once they no longer find it important to identify with their Russian heritage, they will abandon it, except on special Russian holidays. Hispanics, Asians, Native Americans and we African Americans have different entry points into American history. Interestingly enough, we Americans hated the Russians during the cold war; skin color was not even a part of the equation. We all still wince when we hear a Russian accent. Russian immigrants reallize their accents hold them back from achieving the American dream, so they drop their accent along with much of their culture and ethnicity in order to become American. Remember, most Americans are, ethnically, some other people in disguise. Black Americans have had a tough time trying to find the appropriate disguise, since it's not easy to disguise the color of our skin. Italians and Russians dropped their language and accents, and they are in disguise, especially in the American work place. The physical attributes of Black Americans bring the assimilation process to a slow grind, and it is not an easy to change the way this process works, since nobody really owns it.

**"Once you become a part of a society you will be pressed into its processes, especially the assimilation process."**

The assimilation process in America struggles with physical and tangible attributes more than any other parameter that it encounters. The reason why, is simple. Assimilation seeks to change all that is being assimilated and incorporate what it can into the "whole" or as the Borg (from televisions "Star Trek: The Next Generation Series") would say, "The Collective."

I am a Star Trek addict and the most intriguing, yet unnerving episode I ever watched, was the one called, "The Borg." For those of you who are not Star Trek fans, I need to bring you up to speed on the Borg. The Borg are a people who are part human and part machine. Even though the Borg are physically unique separate individuals, they think collectively. What one Borg thinks, they all think. In fact, they do not see themselves as individuals, but as one part of a system. Their ship is shaped like a square cube and they all physically plug into the ship to become part of the ship. A Borg does not speak of itself in any way. It says, **"We** are hungry," or **"We** are hurt," and so on. Oh! By the way! I did not see a Borg of color in any of the television episodes. They all look white, and most of them are male. (Please write me if that was an oversight on my part, for those of you who are fellow trekkies. The exception was the 1996 Star Trek movie, which not only had a Borg Queen, but also at least one Black male Borg.) The Borg assume that anyone who is not assimilated into their "collective" should be destroyed. They are one of the most feared beings in the realm of Star Trek Worlds. A people that are alike in most aspect, especially in their thinking, are the hardest people to defeat. The Borg go out looking for worlds they might assimilate, and destroy those that resist assimilation.

There are great similarities between the Borg collective and the American culture. America also attempts to assimilate other cultures. The difference between the Borg and the Americans is the American culture attracts people from other cultures, and then attempts to make them a part of America. To be fair to the American process of assimilation, it does not act like the Borg assimilation process by immediately destroying what it can't assimilate. The American process makes iterative attempts to assimilate races and cultures of people. It can be very patient in its attempt to assimilate other cultures. It has been attempting to assimilate the Black culture for the last 400 years. Unfortunately, it has changed its approach as to how it wants to assimilate the Black Race down through history.

The American assimilation process allows anyone to become American almost at will. But it does not allow people to participate in the benefits of America unless it is forced to. Americans of color have even more challenges, due to our physical differences. As a result, the process becomes downright contentious for Black Americans. No matter how much the process discriminates; it never stops the assimilating. That is why Black Americans have had such trouble with the penal system. It is a socio-economic tool of assimilation that has been used to weed out so-called bad candidates for assimilation. Because incarceration is so widely used to solve problems that are broader in scope than individual crimes, it continues to decimate Black Americans. This tool often short-circuits steps in the assimilation process, as we will explain later in this chapter.

Unlike the Borg, the American Assimilation process discriminates as to what it chooses to incorporate into the American culture. Also unlike the Borg, the assimilation process does not destroy everything, and not everyone can fully assimilate. Adding racism to assimilation creates obstacles so great as to prevent the full assimilation of a race of people who were born on the American shores. As a result, the Black race have not been allowed to fully enter the American assimilation process.

What we are really talking about is the ethnic cleansing process that affects all cultures that enter America. Again, physical attributes are the hardest attributes of a "race of people" to assimilate. The American culture can easily absorb or wipe out an accent or a language in one short generation. The Asian and Hispanic culture are evidence of how fast this process takes place. If the language goes, so does the artistic nature of their spoken words.

The African language and culture was driven out of Black Americans hundreds of years ago. What replaced it came from the position Black Americans held in the White American households. The African and other Black-based cultural foreign languages were wiped clean in order to make Blacks submit to being chattel property. The ability to keep Black Americans ignorant through oppression created a language based on ignorance. That language became part of the American culture selectively for the Black American slave and evolved later for the Black American poor. If you don't think you know what I am talking about view some of the movies from the 40's and 50's that present Blacks as maids, butlers and nannies.

As we discussed earlier, Black Americans have been here for many generations and were not allowed to assimilate for all the reasons presented above and in chapter one. The process held back its ability to educate a race that it did not want to let progress. The language took on a dialect that the American culture doesn't want and refuses to use. The Ebonic discussions of the Oakland School District, in the words of the Borg, are futile and will be destroyed eventually. Ebonics will linger around the ghettos of America, but it will die in the affluent suburbs of this country. I am a witness of this. I shared earlier how I sent my children to stay with their grandparents for a summer. They came home saying things like, "What it be like" and my daughter started calling my son Bra (with the short "a" sound) short for brother, no not pronounced Bro. They soon dropped all of the little bits of the Ebonic dialect in about two weeks after returning back to their north western schools, which are mainly attended by White middle class Americans, their friends and peers. I am a big proponent of keeping Ebonics in my cultural heritage. No, it should not be taught in schools, and it serves no purpose in the American business culture. For Black people, it is very endearing to use with each other. The assimilation process will eventually wipe it out of my family and the Black community. My kids associate it with being poor and uneducated. This will surely kill it. The same way we wiped out the Italian dialects and accents when they were associated with crime and ignorance.

Another example of where the assimilation process slowed down the acceptance of Blacks into the culture is through our dress. Get this, it will let the ghetto dress become fashionable for school age kids, but by college it is no longer fashionable, it is gone. Sagging pants and those big starter jackets, the citizens of the "hood" have made so popular are all gone by the time students are fully into their college curriculums. However, it let African cultural fashion come into play for Black American Adults: the bright kente' clothes and long flowing dashikis are becoming vogue. I have yet to see a White American fully modeling one of those great yellow and Black African outfits. Sears and J.C. Penny have done their homework, and have added catalogs and displays, that include Black mannequins, which showcase these works of art. This attire can only be worn outside of the workplace for those Black American attempting to climb the corporate ladder.

Often the assimilation process finds ways to steer the Black American away from full participation and convinces us we don't want to be fully assimilated. It was true when I worked for "Big Blue" (IBM). I would not wear a button down collar because it was such a surrender to the corporate culture, which I knew was defined by White America. Now that I am over forty, I look for shirts that only have some type of button down collar. An interesting twist was added to men's clothing during the time when I was writing this section. The "ban collared shirt," became very fashionable. My Black brethren totally incorporate it into their highly fashionable evening attire. But, it wasn't until I saw one of my White colleagues wearing one that I bought my first one. I now have many and I am wearing one as I write this paragraph. These shirts are now well received by all Americans. In my opinion, once they show up on prime time TV or at the movie theaters, they are in. A Black American cultural dress just might blast the American tie out. I have noticed the ban collar to be in the Asian culture as well, but it was Black men who made them stylish and popular here in the USA.

A final note on how the assimilation processes chooses to include and exclude Black American culture. This process is working very well, not as efficiently as we might think, but it is working. Once we Black Americans gained significant access to the education and economic system in America, we became part of defining the process. The old adage is true "in order to change the system you must first become a part of the system," even when it does not want you too! We are a part of the system and the process.

Black Americans are still a long way from controlling or being able to make significant changes to the process. But, Black America is now in a position to truly influence the process. White America spent the last 400 years defining this process and living it. Today, we can better attempt to define what this process should be and how to positively affect America as it progresses toward providing opportunity for all of us. I am confident that we Americans will create a process that will benefit all Americans.

### *What Are The Steps To Fully Assimilating Into The American Culture?*

### Step One - Learn to speak the language.

People quickly learn, in order to be successful in America, you have to speak the language. This is a part of the assimilation process, which is most visible, or should I say most heard by the listening American. For many years the American assimilation process has been wiping out languages and dialects of the immigrant, and it has not discriminated against any particular European immigrant. It wiped out Italian, Irish, Scandinavian, German, and all other languages, dialects or accents that originated in Europe. It has found a formidable foe in the Asian languages, but it is winning that battle as well.

It wiped out the African language immediately due to slavery and through the power White Americans had over early Black Americans. It chose to work on Black Americans in a different fashion, in that it chose to eliminate dialects of Black speak or sometimes called Black slang. It has taken some interesting turns by collecting a lot of Black-speak into the language, and I give rap music the credit for this inclusion through the power of the media. American education continues to slowly assimilate Black-speak, and Black Americans are sounding more and more like Northwestern Americans everyday.

This is a step of the assimilation process that has been very active lately in our society. I must admit it has somewhat shifted its focus from Black Americans to other people who are immigrating into America. At the time of authorship, it appeared to be focusing in on Spanish speaking people due to the large influx of Mexicans coming into America.

**Step Two - Lose your ethnic accent.**

This step is very selective. It focuses on immigrants, and it has been at work since America was only thirteen colonies. This step can be seen as a continuation of step one. It works across generations on European ethnic cultures and the races of color. It seeks to make everyone sound like Northwesterners, or like the newscaster you hear on television every night. CNN and other television and radio news programs are the prime educators, and a big part of this tool. It continues to work on Americans who live in the southern and eastern parts of the United States. It continues to work on the Northeasterners as well.

**Step Three - Gain a source of income.**

This step in the assimilation process is unique to America. It has some very positive features. It seeks to assist those who have trouble obtaining a source of income. We have public assistance and philanthropy that seek to help as many people as they can. This step in the process is easy to obtain for the greater percentage of people that enter the process. The other steps often influence what happens in this step of the process.

A source of income is the reason most people are attracted to this country. It is easy to find at the low economic stratas of our society. Increasing and maintaining this income can often be the challenge. This, however, is one of the most important steps of a culture that is based on capitalism.

**Step Four - Define, gain or adopt a set of beliefs.**

Gaining any set of beliefs will do, but if they are Christian beliefs, the process becomes easier. Churches are often the sanctuaries for the migrating poor people of various cultures. These people come to America because of some unfortunate situation in the motherland of their culture. Most of us have forgotten the boat people that migrated here during and after the Viet Nam War. These people have rapidly assimilated into the American culture up to the point where it has allowed them. Most of these people were brought here and cared for by various Christian Churches. The Russians have been immigrating here over the last ten years, and are brought here and established in the local communities by local churches. Foreigners who adopt the beliefs of the assisting church or agency are more likely to be successful in America than those who go off on their own to set up their own belief system or church.

**Step Five - Become educated in the American thinking process.**

This step, like the language step, might take a generation. A college education from the Philippines or some other third world country doesn't fully encompass the American problem-solving techniques. We can observe how the process works for doctors and lawyers who were educated in foreign lands. These doctors and lawyers often have trouble passing logic exams, which appear in most of our board exams. This is the same education (inference thinking) discussed in the previous chapter on thinking processes.

To be educated in America is to be assimilated into an important part of the culture. To understand the American approach to problem solving is to understand a lot about the American culture. I remember my days in college trying to fully comprehend what America cares about and deciding what I should care about. Education is truly the tool we used to do this. Most Asian cultures understand this step very well. Black Americans struggle to realize how import this step is to the success of the Black race in America. Black Americans are learning to value education as an everyday occurrence. The only sad part about this step in the process is it is a step that is becoming less accessible to Black Americans.

**Step Six - Own a piece of the land.**

Many immigrants use this step to try to bypass other steps in the assimilation process. They are generally not totally successful, but there are times when they are able to assimilate into the culture as much as it allows them to or as much as they want to. Owning a piece of the rock is very important. It is the first step to gaining any kind of wealth in America. Real Estate is still the best investment you can make in America. It is one of the most visible messages you can send to Americans that you care about this country.

Black Americans are learning how to access the financial system in order to execute this step in the process. I must admit, one of the best feelings I have ever experienced – that made me truly feel I was an American – was when I signed the papers to own my first home. It is still the scariest and the most awesome feeling to sign up for a $100,000 or more of debt to purchase a home. When you walk into a home and know that you are the one who is responsible for paying the mortgage you truly become a proud American.

**Final Step - Look like a White American.**

It is hard for many of us to accept that this step exists. Black and White America are often in denial over this step. This step, which has its main basis in the color of the skin, is all but impossible for Black Americans and other people of color. The human mind is quite capable of adapting to any situation it is given. Black Americans go deep with in their mind to find ways to deal with this lack of acceptance based on the color of our skin.

You can quickly make several conclusions as to why Black Americans struggle, and never finish, all the steps to assimilate. Why they are often kept from accomplishing steps 3, 5, 6, and blocked from ever accomplishing the final step. The system is a perpetual system and we Americans simply have learned to live with in it. We constantly change this system, mostly for the better, but sometimes for the worst.

**When a process is inherently discriminative, it is the hardest process to change, no matter how willing the people. These steps are not prescribed by anyone today, but are a part of the practice of an intelligent society."**

## Degrees of Assimilation

Describing steps to assimilation would quickly bring one to question how much do people actually subscribe to this process? There are various degrees of assimilation in America. We started out discussing examples in the earlier part of this chapter. Because the majority culture is White, White-skinned people of any other culture can assimilate quicker and easier than Black-skinned people. Earlier, we described how Russians are starting to assimilate into the American culture. Many Russian immigrants are White. This enables them to automatically cross the biggest hurdle to assimilation. Then they must learn the language, and start an education in the American thinking process. Learning the language is not that hard of a task for many foreigners. Learning to think American is very difficult, even for a White Russian. If you are coming from a culture that is very different in its political ideology and you are not willing to give it up, it can be harder than almost any other part of the assimilation process.

### *Do Black Americans Really Want To Assimilate?*

Black Americans often think they don't want to assimilate, and are often confused when trying to integrate. When a process has been designed to inherently work against assimilation, it is easy to think it is not necessary or, more importantly, not worth it. Black Americans definitely want to assimilate, and they demonstrate this each and everyday. They go to their perspective jobs, and they do what is required of them. They often feel that more is required of them, because of who they are. These expectations don't factor in the limits of what they can become, based on what society will allow them to accomplish.

Black Americans continue to change their clothing and other things to make them look like "Americans." They also continue to influence American culture in very positive ways. They continue to be the best entertainers, athletes, cooks, and housekeepers. Now with the opportunity to gain an education, they are becoming some of the nations top lawyers, engineers, accountants and, of course, politicians. They are assimilating, wouldn't you agree? They don't like to think that they are assimilating, but that is the only true path to the American dream that we are all seeking. And, Black Americans are well into the pursuit of the American dream.

As I stated earlier, the question is no longer do they want to assimilate, it is how fast does it take to get through the process? The world will continue to progress and Black Americans will continue to progress, whether or not we think assimilation is good or bad. They will continue to be a part of the American cultural assimilation process by participating in it, by changing it, and, someday, being accepted by it.

### *Where Do Black Americans Fit In To The America Of Today?*

Black Americans are constantly trying to decide where they fit in America. Although the process was set up nearly 400 years ago, its barriers to letting Black Americans participate make it difficult for Black Americans to want to fit in. But Black people are a major part of America, and they – and it – now have no choice but to find the proper place for Black Americans.

A prediction: It will take another full century before America is mostly colorblind. The education system will wipe out the intellectual difference between Black and White America. The capitalistic nature of our society has already begun to assimilate the Black dollar into the economy of America. By this, I mean, White corporate America has started planning to get the Black dollar in its boardrooms. This is an important change in the way America does business. Corporate America continues to seek ways to get the Black Dollar. (Currently, Black Americans represent $400 million in purchasing power.) This will lead to Blacks learning to earn and value the dollar, which will lead to a greater increase in Black wealth. Greater wealth will lead to more educated Black Americans, and a better educated Black American will obtain more knowledge of how to gain ownership of America. If you understood what was discussed in the earlier parts of this chapter, you have correctly figured that the assimilation process is starting to work for Black America. Profound change processes, such as assimilation, are very hard to change and tremendously hard to control. We can create them easily, but they are hard to stop once in motion.

America will continue to assimilate Black America whether it wants to or not. The process started a long time ago, and it will never be stopped without some significant paradigm anomalies.

The probability of destroying American culture is higher than the probability of stopping the assimilation of Blacks into America: Most of the Blacks that were born of America are truly patriotic Americans, and would die for America.

White Americans must continue to seek a true understanding of what it means to assimilate the Black American culture. White Americans have already lost a significant battle — they have lost the wonderful richness of the various cultures of Europe. Maintaining the ethnic cultural inventory from the Black American community and other ethnic communities in America is how we will sustain the entire American culture. That is what will continue to make America the truly beautiful.

One final note is that all Americans have a responsibility to each other to create an America that includes all of its parts. Failure to do so means none of its parts will be truly successful. The hand cannot work unless the arm is working properly. Sure, you could say, if an eye offends you, pluck it out, but, in this day of knowledge as power, wouldn't it be easier to restore the eye to its healthiest state?

# Chapter
# 5

## Chapter Five - Are Blacks As Talented As They Appear?

$\mathcal{M}$ost Whites have been introduced to Blacks through some media talent, news story, or sports figure. In the second chapter of this book you were introduced to several Black Americans who have made significant accomplishments in American history. George Washington Carver did amazing things with the peanut. Dr. Charles Drew developed a way to make blood plasma, still our most life-enhancing invention. A modern day contributor to the American high quality of life was Dr. Martin Luther King, Jr. who was responsible for the strides we have made to live peacefully in America. Maya Angelo's words live in our society. Our modern day technical and artistic talents are numerous as well. Due to the way American history has been presented, we have not recognized some of our biggest contributors to everyday life, and many of them are Black Americans.

Black Americans made significant contributions to some of the most significant inventions of our times. Lewis H. Latimer was the draftsman who assisted Thomas Edison with the final design of the light bulb. It was Latimer's research that led to an inexpensive, long-lived carbon filament that was patented in 1882. Yes, he was a Black man. He was also very instrumental in helping Alexander Graham Bell achieve his patent for the telephone. Latimer drew the critically precise drawings necessary to gain the patent.

Black Americans have continued to excel in almost everything they have been allowed to do. Given the opportunity, we will excel, and sometimes far exceed, our White counterparts due to the drive that comes from being oppressed as a people. This is not do to some latent chromosome or some special potion we rub on our bodies. This is due to the same thing I have talked about in the earlier chapters of this book. We, like all other Americans will take advantage of the opportunities afforded us.

For some reason, America has allowed Black Americans to excel in sports. Seventy percent of all football players are Black Americans. We have dominated the sports of basketball, baseball, football, and track and field and now the sacred game of golf. The reason should be a big surprise. When a person is only allowed access to a limited number of sports, he or she becomes very focused and determined to succeed in that sport. That determination leads to excellence. White Americans will respond, or should I say perform, in the same way, especially those who have not had a silver spoon in their mouths. In this chapter I would like to examine some of those individuals who have been declared the best in their areas of expertise.

### Michael Jordan Can't Be That Good, Can He?

Are Blacks superior to other races when it comes to physical prowess and athletic ability? The answer is Yes and No!! Yes, they can be the best athletes in the world and no it is not just due to some special muscle structure God has only given to Black people. I don't believe there is any doubt in any American's mind that Michael Jordan is the greatest basket ball player in the world. In fact, I believe if we asked this question in any country, in any part of the world, we would get a similar answer. Michael Jordan is the greatest basketball player in the world. But how did he get so great? Did Black superiority allow Michael Jordan to become great? Is it his African ancestry from the tall Watusi Tribe in Africa? Is it a physical make-up that White Americans don't have? There is really one simple answer to most of these questions, and that answer is OPPORTUNITY.

America attempts to provide opportunity for anyone to become almost anything they want to be, if they are willing to understand how America works. A Black person could only become as great as Michael Jordan in America. Are there White players that are better at shooting basketballs than Michael? Yes! Are there white players who can jump higher than Michael? Yes! There are today and there more certainly will be in the future, Black and White athletes who are better than Michael at doing everything he does and we may or may not ever hear about them. Michael Jordan is a Black American (and I emphasize **American**) who has had the opportunity to capitalize on his skills and ability. His Airness deserves everything he has earned in this great capitalistic society we live in. But, how did this happen?

Anatomically, Michael is like a million other Black and White people. He is tall, and has long legs, two eyes, ten fingers, and a brain. Does he have special muscles in his legs that White people don't have? Yes, due to the fact that he developed his leg muscles for more than twenty years through training, practice, and hard work to become a star. In the same way, Scottie Hamilton developed his legs to execute the jumps that allow him to do triple axles on the ice. There are many Black kids who could grow up to be as good as Scottie, if given the opportunity. Michael, like a lot of other young Black kids, went down to the school playground with a basketball, probably furnished by the school, and played the game. Michael and many other American kids became very good at sports because there is an opportunity to participate and learn sports in American schools. Add to that natural ability and a push from parents to be good at sports because it's a way to get a college scholarship, and you have the making of an American superstar. It happened for White kids long before Michael Jordan got to play on his high school basketball team. Long before Jackie Robinson was allowed to play in major league baseball. Long before Arthur Ashe was allowed to play tennis at Wimbledon. He is Mr. American Basketball.

# Chapter 5

## *A Great Black Golfer, Tiger Woods, You Must Be Kidding?*

During the period I was writing this chapter I had a great American experience. What I really had was an opportunity to witness history in the making. Tiger Woods, a 20-year-old, won the 1996 U.S. Amateur Championship. Not only did he win it, but he won it for the third time, a feat never accomplished before. Tiger Woods' skin is not White, and in that lies the importance of my experience. Tiger happens to be 50% Asian (Thai and Chinese), 25% Black, and the rest Native American and White, a multiracial fellow, according to his parents. Tiger calls himself a Cablanasian, in order to capture all the richness of his ethnic heritages. In America, if he were a dog, we would call him a mutt. But in America, if you look Black, you will be treated as Black.

Tiger looks Black. When he was a kid in elementary school, he was tied to a tree by his fellow students because he was the only Black kid in the group. After being tied to the tree a sign was placed on him that read "nigger." The other kids than threw rocks at him and drew blood. Tiger went home devastated. Even though this may have been child's play, it was an experience that neither Tiger nor his parents viewed positively. Tiger does not appear to have any major hang-ups from this experience, but deep in his guts he is quite aware of what it means to be Black in America, even as the wonderkind of America's real favorite pastime, golf.

I had the opportunity to talk to Tiger's father, Earl Woods, as we watched his son make golf history. Meeting Earl Woods made this experience unique and purposeful. He took time to share with me how Tiger had risen above the color of his skin to become the best amateur golfer ever. Earl said he took golf and made it a learning tool for teaching Tiger about life. He told me how he and his wife Kultida, whom I also had the pleasure to meet, worked with Tiger since he was four years old to help him prepare for the day he would win his third U.S. Amateur Championship. He told me how the White golf-pro at the golf club near their home would take time to teach Tiger and the other kids the fundamentals of how to swing the club. Kultida would drive Tiger to the course in the morning, and pick him up in the evening. In between that time, Tiger practiced, making him the champion he is today. This all adds up to an American opportunity, which undoubtedly has led to Tiger's and his parent's great success.

But wait, it gets better! I saw Tiger the first day of the championship and there were only a couple hundred people watching him. I happen to be one of the few Blacks to come and watch him. Several young kids, mostly White, asked me if I was related to him. People kept staring at me, and, for a moment, I felt I was sharing in Tiger, Kultida and Earl's glory. I saw him several more times, and the crowd continued to swell. I heard White women talking about how handsome he is, and White men discussing every aspect of his game and how superb a golfer he is. I was very proud to be Black and American. On the day Tiger won the championship, it was reported that there were 14 thousand people who had come to see him and I am here to tell you that only about a hundred of them were Black people. There were many Asians and I heard several of them discussing whether or not I was somebody famous just because they saw me at the golf course when history was made. On this day, I felt that there was much hope and that the divide between Black Americans and White Americans had closed slightly. If you missed this historic event or you are reading this book a long time after it was written, Tiger Woods turned pro three days after he won the championship.

It has been reported that Tiger signed product endorsement contracts in the range of $40 - $60 million dollars for Nike and Titlelist, the world's biggest golf ball and accessories manufacturer. He was still signing deals the day I wrote this paragraph. Nike's first commercial featured Tiger from the time he was four up until the day he turned pro. It highlighted Tiger's career and uniquely weaved into the story how race is an important factor in Tiger's future as a golf professional. As a Black man I thought it was tastefully done, even if Nike's goal was simply to make money.

One final note about Tiger: in his first year as a golf professional he won the Masters with no other golfer within 12 strokes of his lead. He was featured on Nightline in a story that discussed how important a step America was making by recognizing the skills and talents of a young golfer of color and how he would affect America's favorite pass time for years to come. I am sure you know that Tiger is not the first Black golfer to play professional golf, but he is the first to make millions of dollars without ever winning a professional tournament. More than that, he was recognized for his potential. This is a significant step in increasing our understanding about the relationships between Black and White Americans in a sport that has mainly been a White American sport. If we Americans offer each other the opportunity to participate in all aspects of society, our society will be greatly enhanced for all of us. It was reported that Tiger made in excess of $150 million his first year as a professional golfer. His peers picked him as golfer of the year. He finished number one in earnings for the year of 1997. Now that's an American dream come true.

### *Who Was This Florence Griffith Joyner Lady?*

She was just one of the most talented black female athletes of the 80's and 90's. In the 1988 Olympics she clocked in at 23.5 mph in the 100 meter. She continued to run track and became one of the prettiest faces used to sell milk. Her physical abilities afforded her the opportunity to use her mental abilities as well. Shortly before her untimely death and during the final writing of this book, she was sought to model and speak for all kinds of organizations and corporations. She was an outstanding ambassador for America to the entire world.

### *Michael Jackson Is He Really Black?*

Michael, in recent times has been amongst the most controversial of celebrity figures. He continues to struggle with an identity crisis, at least according to what we see in the media. I remember when he was just a cute Black American kid along with his other brothers and sisters. I struggle with how he presents himself today, but I am careful not to judge him too harshly. Michael changed the way we view music in this country. I still get all goose bumpy when I hear him sing "When I Had You." He was rapidly approaching forty when I was writing this chapter, and was still being referred to as the King of Pop. If you are reading this book ten years after its copyright date, he is probably still making music, and continuing to define what we hold so dear in the American culture. Michael has been the highest paid musical talent for many years, and is still as capable of selling out a concert in America as he is in selling out an event in any other part of the world.

Is Michael one of the best singers in the country? Not in my book, but he most certainly is the best packaged singing entertainer I have ever seen. He dances with so much charisma, even if you don't like him, he will still mesmerize you with his multidirectional pelvic gestures. He is a super star of this day and age and will continue to entertain people for sometime to come. He is an American music legend in his own time.

### Is Oprah As Outstanding As She Appears?

Oprah, who at the time of authorship, made over $190,000,000 in one year (1997) of work and investments is the highest paid actress – or actor – of our time. I think you would admit we have a class act that has transcended all races and walks of life. She just may be the most popular face in the world, sharing that honor with the King of Pop and/or his Airness.

She has purchased her own television and Production Company, Harpo Productions, and is the first Black woman or man to have this accomplishment under her belt. She continues to use her show to inform America about itself and its day-to-day life. She is a tremendous American philanthropist and often helps others to enjoy life.

Chapter 5

## *What About This Denzel Washington Character ? Can He Really Act?*

This man is so talented that it is not amazing how many of you White American women have declared him one of the most sexist men in America. He is gripping in every performance I have ever seen him act. He takes over the screen, no matter who is casted with him, and he continues to be one of the biggest box offices draws of his time.

Denzel transcends time by being allowed to play non-stereotypic parts in the movies he chooses to work in. He is almost always in a leadership role and we Black Americans need to see ourselves lead more than we need to see anything else. Our role models are too shallow for the most part, and our community leaders are few and far between. Black Americans are starving for leadership and role models. All our major advocacy agencies are struggling for good leaders. We have very few people to act as role models for our youth.

Denzel suffers from being Black. He does not make the money of a Tom Hanks or a Jim Carey, who are also multitalented individuals. But in my humble opinion he gives Hanks and Carey a run for the money and he continues to be the actor that makes a character come to life right before your very eyes. He has become the greatest American military character actor of this century.

## *Dr. William Cosby - Is He The Most Successful Comedian/ Businessman In America?*

Bill Cosby has entertained America for the last 30 years, and was one of the most successful sitcom comedians of the 60's, 70's, 80's and 90's. He was the highest paid TV actor for over five years and kept the NBC network in the number one spot for most of the years he stared in the Cosby Show. He has recorded over 25 albums. He is as funny and witty as a comedian, and is equally as good as a husband and a father.

It is estimated that Dr. Cosby makes $500,000 a week when he performs in Las Vegas. His annual income averages about $50 million a year. He and his wife Camille have donated as much as $20 million dollars to Historically Black Colleges and Universities.

Bill Cosby is an author and has a Ph.D. in Education. He is not perfect, since we know he admitted to being unfaithful to his wife as a young man. He continues to serve as a great role model to Black American men, women and children, as well as all other Americans.

### *Is Ken Griffey, Jr. As Good As His Father Ken Griffey, Sr.?*

Ken Griffey, Jr. and Ken Griffey, Sr. were a father and son team who hit back-to- back home runs while being members of the Seattle Mariners. Ken Griffey, Jr. is now one of the highest paid baseball players in the world. He is noted for hitting home runs in eight consecutive games tying the major league record. He has continuously been a great role model to kids all over America.

### *Who Is Warren Moon?*

A very talented quarterback, who led the Houston Oilers to the Superbowl and remembered to share the spotlight with his young son. He was a star quarterback at the University of Washington, leading the Huskies to a Rose Bowl title in 1978. At the time this is being written, he is still playing football for the Seattle Seahawks for millions of dollars each year that he plays. I attended the University of Washington during the time Warren led the Huskies to the 1978 Rose Bowl.

### *Earl Graves - Is He An Entertainer Or An Athlete Too!*

No, Absolutely not! Some might mistake him for an entertainer, because his products do provide entertainment. To answer the question, Earl is a businessman first, and has built a media empire that has kept professional Black Americans informed for the last twenty years. His major product is Black Enterprise Magazine, which is an up-to-date, powerfully written, information-laden tool for the Black American business professional. Earl Graves is the publisher of this great vehicle of information. A lot of the data for this book was researched and presented by Black Enterprise writers. Earl has continued to convene economists, business professionals, and experts to analyze and present details about Black American Business practices and success. In 1997 Earl wrote a book about how to be successful in business if you are Black. If you would like to gain more understanding about Black American business accomplishments, subscribe to Black Enterprise. I must warn you that Black Enterprise reads very much like Time, Fortune, or any of the other business magazines that have become American business tools of the Twenty and Twenty First Centuries.

# Chapter
# 6

## Chapter Six - Has Every Black American Had A Bad Experience With The "System" In America? Are All Those Complaints Invalid?

$\mathcal{T}$he answer is no! But proportionally, Black Americans continue to have more negative experiences with police and government (collectively known as "the system") than any other race of people in America. Some of you may remember former Governor of Virginia L. Douglas Wilder, the first Black American governor in the United States. At the time of this writing, Governor Wilder was still the only Black American ever to serve as governor in the United States. According to an article in Ebony Magazine, August 1996, Governor Wilder, who is a very distinguished looking man between 50 and 60 years of age, was on his way home after he had just finished giving a speech at Duke University. At the Raleigh-Durham Airport he walked through the metal detector and the buzzer went off. He went through the metal detector again after emptying his pockets, and then a third time. It finally dawned on him that he was wearing suspenders, so he told the security person, who was a white man, his suspenders had triggered the alarm. The security man, who for some reason became angry, grabbed him, pushed him, and started to choke him. This incident resulted in the former Governor Wilder suing the airport for $5 million dollars and settling for an undisclosed amount. The governor was quoted as saying, "It shouldn't matter whether I am a former Governor or not, a human being shouldn't be treated this way."

# Chapter 6

This happens more times than most Blacks or Whites would like to think. That is, because of the color of our skin, we Blacks are treated poorly by the authorities. In the chapter titled, "Is Black American Thinking Different Than White American Thinking," I shared an example of how thought processes can make people come to very racist conclusions. Let me share a personal experience, which fits under the complaint column.

I picked up a newspaper on Saturday, May 17, 1997, as I do every Saturday morning. The Oregonian, the local newspaper in Portland, Oregon, had a large picture of President Bill Clinton embracing a very elderly Black man. The headline read "Tuskegee men receive late apology." After reading the story I was absolutely astonished at what the article conveyed. The story explained, in 1932 the U.S. government conducted an experiment on 600 Black men. The project was called, "The Tuskegee syphilis experiment." It was one of the most disgraceful human experiments of our times. Today there are five surviving members.

According to the news article, the experiment entailed using 600 mostly uneducated Black men in Alabama who agreed to participate in a study in exchange for free meals, medical care, and burial expenses. What was not told until 1972, was that 399 men who suffered from syphilis weren't treated, even with the advent of a cure called penicillin in the 1940's. Many of the men died of the disease and its complications. Some of their wives and babies were affected. The case has had lingering and harmful affects on many Blacks who already distrust the mostly White American led medical establishment and who shun treatment and participation in potentially beneficial studies. And you wonder why Black Americans think AIDS is a genocidal attempt by White Americans to wipe out the Black Race.

*"What was done cannot be undone, but we can end the silence. We can stop turning our heads away, we can look at you, in the eye, and finally say, on behalf of the American people, what the United States government did was shameful."*
*President Clinton*

A response by one of the Tuskegee men:
*"The wounds that were inflicted upon us cannot be undone. I'm saddened today to think of those who did not survive and whose families will forever live with the knowledge that their death and suffering was preventable."*

Herman Shaw,
94-year-old survivor

The above story is very healing for many Black Americans, including me. We humans are strange, no matter what our color or ethnic heritage, we all simply want people to know our story. President Clinton started a tremendous healing process by airing this whole tragic ordeal. This is a perfect example of what America should be doing to heal the relations between White and Black America.

While attending school at the University of Washington in Seattle, I rode the bus home daily. Often I would stop on my way home in downtown Seattle to see my wife at her place of employment. One day, I got off the bus and was walking down the street in broad day light, and a police squad car pulled up and two officers got out of the car. One of the officers was Asian and one was White. The White officer was very aggressive and grabbed me, spun me around and pushed me up against the wall. I was carrying a backpack full of books. The books were on all types of sciences ranging from Physics to Calculus, necessary for one who is majoring in engineering and minoring in physics, which I tried to explain to the officers who were detaining me. The White officer pulled my bag away and gave it to the Asian officer, who promptly looked inside and put the bag down. The White officer than begin to frisk me in good old routine fashion. He was quite rough with me. Needless to say, I was so taken by surprise. I could hardly speak, which is a very rare state for me. After convincing himself and his partner that I was not armed or carrying anything of a dangerous nature, he pushed me towards his partner, who was noticeably gentler and a lot less aggressive with me. They put me in the squad car, and drove me several blocks to a branch office of a bank. I was as quiet as a mouse during this episode. I watch movies, too, and was not about to give them a reason to hurt me. When we arrived at the bank, the White officer escorted me to the window of the bank, and gestured to the lady in the bank to look at me. She immediately shook her head no. For the first time during this experience, I let myself relax.

The cops started to apologize for the inconvenience and I immediately went off on them. I believe I said, " You do not treat citizens like they are animals." I turned to the White officer, who looked almost as young as I was, and said, do you know who pays your salary? Which I wasn't doing much of, as I was collecting my G.I. Bill while going to school. Before he could answer my question, I turned to his Asian counterpart and said, "Give me your badge number." I was slightly kinder to the Asian officer, I guess, because I was subconsciously reciprocating for his gentler approach in handling me. I ranted and raved for a few minutes longer as they returned my books back to me. I started into them again, repeating that you do not treat people like they are guilty. They both tried to calm me down by offering an explanation of why they had to be so rough with me during the frisking. One said, you might have been armed. I finally regained my composure and walked away from them still spouting off at them.

I never filed a complaint, but I will never forget what happened to me. What was most disturbing and haunting was the thought of the women at the bank saying, "Yes, that's him." Whites often think Blacks look a lot alike. I thought of how I might have been convicted, and sent to some awful prison simply because I was Black. I am very dark skinned, and I believe the darker we are, the more we are feared by Whites, and the worse we are treated in these situations. It is an experience I hope no one will ever have to experience. But, I know it happens to Black people on a daily basis, truly out of proportion when compared to the percentage of Whites who face similar treatment.

Here is another story I read in Ebony. Mayor Sharpe James of Newark, New Jersey told how he has always been an avid fisherman. He purchased a boat that was 42 feet long. The White salesman offered to take him out into the channel in his new boat. (Incidentally, I don't think it is very likely you would find a Black salesman selling 42 foot long boats. That is not an experience many Black people would have, due to their inability to purchase such a boat. Whites who could never afford to purchase one of the boats would be more likely than Blacks to sell luxury boats. Even I can't get over the thought of a fellow Black brother buying a 42 foot boat. I myself have a 14 foot boat, and I do not see many Black Americans with a boat the size of mine, let alone a 42 foot boat. It is not that many Black American can't afford the 14 foot boat, it's just that they don't have the life experiences that would make them want to purchase one.) Back to the story. As the Mayor and the salesman were going through the channel, the state troopers came along. They waved at 40 or more people, who all appeared to be white, in the boats that passed before the one the mayor was buying. As soon as they saw the mayor, they fired up their sirens and flashed their lights. They boarded his boat and asked him where he stole it. The Mayor told them he had bought it, and they asked to see the papers. He was about to get the documentation out when the salesman walked out of the cabin. The trooper recognized the salesman, said "Oh Bob, if you sold him the boat then he must be okay." What is ironic about this story, is they never looked at his papers after the White salesman appeared, and silently vouched for this esteemed mayor who happens to be a Black American. These events don't just affect me and you, they affect all the people around us and the relationships that make up the quality of our lives.

As a Black father in America, I have first-hand experience with how the system can be unfair. I came home very early one day, when my daughter, a second grader in a private school in the Seattle area, had this experience. We enrolled her in the school associated with the church we attended. My daughter truly enjoyed going to the school, except for this one life-impacting experience that my entire family will never forget. My daughter's second grade teacher decided to take all of the kids out in front of a big hotel to sell candy. I believe the teacher rotated the kids and positioned them so they would all have their chance to sell a bar of candy. My seven-year-old daughter was the only Black kid in the class and the only kid that did not sell a bar of candy. She came home devastated and upset. Watching her tell the story was very heart wrenching. She said, nobody wanted to buy candy from her, because she was Black. My wife and I were silent for a long time as we looked at each other, and started to question my daughter on how she had come to those conclusions. We asked questions like, did you ask people to buy your candy? Her answer was yes. Were there lots of people passing on the sidewalk where you were standing? She said yes, and they bought candy from her classmates who were standing next to her. We tried to come up with all sorts of rationalizations that might have changed her conclusions. We were not very successful. We decided, right or wrong, not to confront the teacher, or make a big deal out of the incident. My wife cried with my daughter. At the time of writing this book, my daughter is about seventeen-years-old and still attends schools that have predominantly White American student bodies. Most of her friends are White, and she seems to manage just fine. I still worry as to whether or not she is getting fair treatment. I have convinced myself that she is better for her previous experiences as a second grader.

I continued to rationalize how people of any race or ethnicity could decide to buy from a kid that looked like them, and not from one who didn't. Being a consultant on race, I know it happens every day of the week, and at a very unconscious level most of the time. If I were to tell these people that they were making these decisions unconsciously and the effect they were having on other people, they would most certainly argue with me and think such conclusions were ridiculous.

A similar incident happened when my son was eleven-years-old. As I have mentioned in earlier chapters, my family and I live in suburban communities with significantly large White populations. My young, fifth-grader son went to a public school that is made up of a predominantly White American student body. Ninety-nine point one percent of the time, my kids enjoy wonderful relationships with their fellow students who are White. One day, my wife was called by the teacher to tell her that our son had stolen some candy out of her desk drawer, and passed it out to the other students in the class. The teacher informed my wife that she kept candy in her drawer to reward students for good behavior. My wife was very much disturbed that my young son had stolen candy from a teacher. This was the ultimate embarrassment for her, as she talked with the teacher and profusely apologized for the actions of our son. She was literally ready to strangle him for such behavior.

When my son arrived home from school, he did not attempt to deny what he had done. What was so ironic was the pride he displayed for what he had done, which left us baffled at first. He admitted he did it and was ready for any punishment we wanted to give to him. He then proceeded to explain his side of the story. He said, he felt his teacher was very unfair in giving all of the other students two pieces of candy, while giving him only one. He said he thought she only gave him one piece of candy because he was Black. In talking with the teacher, we found no real evidence to support his conclusion. In fact we found this teacher to be a caring and nurturing teacher, who appeared to really like our son. She had always been very good at taking time to tell us of our son's needs and progress in her class. What was interesting to me was how he chose to remedy the problem. We had a long discussion about this incident. My son is a very carefree spirit, and is rarely rattled by what he might think to be injustice of some other nature or some other bad experience. My wife and I never came to any rational conclusion of why our son thought the teacher was being unfair, and what led to his remedy of the problem. I must admit, to this day I continue to wonder what triggered this emotional response in my son. There are not many positive thoughts that I can take away from an experience of this nature, and I am convinced my son found the whole experience to be very unpleasant.

We had long talks with my son and older daughter about how to handle and control these thoughts in the future. I looked upon the whole experience, as one my family should learn from.

What I hoped my son and my daughter finally carried away from these experiences was, do not return injustice with more injustice. We did punish my son, and were careful to explain to him that we were not punishing him for his analysis and conclusion of the experience, but for the bad behavior. I must say that these are normal experiences for most Black American parents who have children in interracially mixed schools. As a parent, I would not want it any other way. I do hope one day that Black children will never have to face such negative experiences while they are receiving their primary education. I must also admit, I think this day is still a long way off. But it is coming.

As a parent I am sad that my children have had experiences that will be remembered for the rest of their lives. What I hope will happen is that they will continue to be the well-rounded people that they have become, and continue to have friends that are from all walks of life.

## The Christian Affect

Promise Keepers is Christian organization that was established to unite men through vital relationships so they can become godly influences in the world. Promise Keepers are committed to keeping seven promises. These promises are aimed at enhancing the Christian man's walk with God. The sixth promise is the most pertinent to the subject matter of this book:

"A Promise Keeper is committed to reach beyond any racial and denominational barrier to demonstrate the power of biblical unity."

Based on this promise, there is a movement within Promise Keepers Organization to bring about racial healing in America in the form of reconciliation. Racial reconciliation is becoming one of the main themes and focus for these Christian men. I, for one, am very impressed with some of the literature they have put forth and the activities they have initiated.

I was reading one of their magazines entitled, "Men of Action" the February 1997 issue about a story told by some of their organizers. The story explains a few organizers were in Queens, New York. They were picked up by another organizer who was from Pennsylvania. He is a Black man who was born and raised in this part of New York and was acting as their host and guide. As written by David Halbrook, the editor of the newsletter, they drove throughout the city in a black Jeep Cherokee. They drove through east Harlem, past ruddy brownstones and flea markets, past the Apollo Theatre near where their Black host's son was killed a few years back. As they past the tragic landmark, the driver sighed, "the best day of my life, was when I got my family out of this city." About that time, a police car lurched forward and followed the Promise Keepers' Jeep. He pulled them over, and jumped out of the car, pistol in hand. He started to interrogate the driver about where he was going and what was he doing. Calmly the driver, who appeared to be familiar with the routine, explained the journey. He explained that they were in town for the Promise Keepers' rally. The officer then looked in at the other passengers and saw they were wearing shirts with the Promise Keepers' logo. The officer then relaxed, and bid them a nice evening. The White organizers couldn't believe what they had just experienced.

When they arrived at their hotel, they attempted to encourage their fellow Black brother in Christ. The White Promise Keepers stated they understood. But in fact, didn't have a clue about what it was like, to be harassed by the police, simply because of the color of their skin. They knew they were all middle-class white men who had no way to relate to what a Black man feels when he is faced with this treatment in his life. The only reason for these negative experiences was the color of his skin. As David wrote, that night they caught a glimpse of a man's recurring nightmare.

# Chapter 6

It is very hard to understand what it is like to be treated as a non-equal in the country that we love. It is not unusual to be stopped by the police in certain parts of town if you are not White. I am sure the driver of the Cherokee had been stopped many times before. It can be very disheartening to be a Black American. The White Promise Keepers had no idea that anyone in America had to endure this kind of treatment.

You might ask, why would the police act in this manner? The answer is, they are trained to be suspicious of everyone. They are taught Black people commit more crimes on a percentage basis than other people do. The police of America are trained to keep the peace and, if at all possible, prevent crime before it happens. They are often over zealous about their work when it comes to people of color. Often, out of fear, they are more suspicious of Blacks and other ethnic minorities than of Whites. This has indeed become a part of our culture and will continue to be a part of our culture for some time to come. Can we change some of this unwanted behavior? You bet!

It takes a lot of education and interaction between the Black and White race in order to change this kind of police behavior. The police are simply a reflection of what our society believes as a whole. You may want to review the statistics in chapter one again. They point out how unfair Black American's experience can be in America. Yes, it is based on the historical experiences of the past. Yes, it is a perpetual experience in our day-to-day lives in America. Yes, it will take time to overcome some of these unfortunate social norms that have been built into our culture. No, I do not find the need to place blame, but I do find the need to understand the nature of the problem and then seek a pertinent solution.

Unfortunately, the solution is not a simple one, but if we keep working on reconciling our differences that are based on the color of our skin, we will solve this problem in America. I applaud Promise Keepers, and consider myself among its members and brothers.

## *What Can White Americans Do To Stop Some Of Those Bad Experiences For Black Americans?*

If you have come this far into this book, and you didn't turn here first, you are well on you way to the answer to the question posed in this section's title. It is so important that White Americans get a serious passion to truly make this country the best place in the world to live for all. Is the burden on you for the quality of life Black Americans live? Only if you are willing to accept the challenge. But if you choose not to accept the challenge, you should stop reading this book now, and get on with your life and never think about Black people again. If you still feel the need to take on this challenge of making America the best place in the world to live, you have made me a happy person.

Find a Black person and make him or her a study project for a period of time. Please don't let them know you are doing this, or you will have failed at your project. This project can be as simple or as complicated as you are willing to make it. You can simply observe this individual or, if you like, you may want to study several Black people. I do this all the time for all kinds of people. But then, you would expect that of a person who makes it his business to know how people think, relate, work, play, and live together.

I think when people take time to observe what they have not really understood, they quickly realize what disservice they have done to others. More importantly, they realize the disservice they have done to themselves. You will hear me say this several times throughout this book, people are the most fascinating subject to other people, because we never fully understand each other. We try hard to understand others by comparing others to ourselves. When race and ethnicity are added to this process, it is difficult to make these comparisons accurately. Our goal – conscious or not – is to make everyone just like us. We believe that no other people can match the accomplishments of Americans. But when we examine our own American culture, and try to apply these same principles, we find we cannot judge ourselves. This leads to the racial strife we experience between White and Black America. We are only able to recognize what the solution is when we are able to remove ourselves from the picture. Once we can critically analyze our role in this reconciliatory process, we can move the whole process forward and start to really understand one another.

*Summary Analysis:* Why can't we judge ourselves? Is it because we don't understand all of us? Because of the assimilation process, we try to make everyone like ourselves. But different races and ethnicity make this difficult to do. In fact, it's difficult to recognize that we have this thought process, so we need to distance ourselves from our normal environment and learn about the environment other racial and ethnic groups live in. This will give us a greater understanding of them and of ourselves. Only when we can critically analyze ourselves, can we really start to understand each other."

# Chapter
# 7

## Chapter Seven - Can There Be Sustainable Social-Economic Development for Black America?

*T*his is at least a $400 billion dollar question and I am going to start off by giving you a 25-cent answer. The social-economic situation is continuing to improve for Black Americans in America. The news here is truly good news, but progress is a lot slower than we all would like it to be, and this question has so many other component questions. We shall ask some of those component questions, and attempt to answer a few of them as we move through this chapter. Are Black Americans gaining more access to capital in America? Is the education system fully available to Black Americans? Are Black Americans creating wealth in our capitalistic society? Is reparation truly a solution to enhance the economic outlook for Black Americans? What does economic development mean to Black Americans?

As you read through this chapter, think about the Black Americans that are a part of your world who are probably the first generation of educated Black Americans. They have not had centuries of experience to help solidify their economic progress, although they are gaining this experience rapidly. Cultures with role models will gain this experience very quickly. But, the role model available to Black Americans is the White American himself. Remember this is a role model, which for hundreds of years would not allow Black Americans to imitate him. Because of this, Black Americans now often reject this role model. This greatly slows down Black Americans' assimilation. (Role-modeling is covered in the chapter on solutions.) With more time and increased opportunities, the recurring, important issue to Black Americans is economics. What does economic development mean to Black Americans?

There is one thing we must understand – American society is not built on fairness to all people. Let's be as honest as we can with ourselves. We Americans like to think we live to be fair to all participants of our society. But the truth is, we look out for number one first. Not only do we believe and practice this, we fully subscribe to the notion of "It is out there, so go out there, and get it for yourself." Clarence Thomas made a statement in this vein during his Supreme Court confirmation hearings, when he talked about the "boot strap" approach he took to get where he had that day. I have heard myself make statements that fit in with this line of thinking. I like to tell people--"You should set goals for yourself! Make a plan and stick to it--when I myself don't have a fully thought-out set of goals or action plan for my own day-to-day living. Does all this rhetoric work? Yes, for the most part. But it does not work for everyone. We can't all be equal in a capitalistic society. The problem with this American line of thinking is that we don't all start out from the same economic start-gate. We don't begin with the same knowledge, the same experience, and a new word I am adding to my vocabulary, the same resources. Resources are necessary to be successful in America.

Hugh Price, President of the National Urban League, in his introduction of "Building A 21$^{st}$ Century Community: The State Of Black America 1996," had this to say:

"If America is to do well in the competition, all groups in American society must be in good social and economic health. All Americans must be equipped—and encouraged—to contribute to our nation's economic well being."

From a resource standpoint, how do you classify Black Americans when it comes to socio-economics in America? Utilizing data that has been compiled by the Urban League in the 1996 State of Black America and U.S. Census data, I present the following information.

## Lower Economic Class Of Black Americans

Approximately 30.6% of Black Americans are living at or below the poverty level as compared to 9.4% of White Americans. There are many Blacks who have climbed up to this level of wealth, or poverty depending on your perspective, in the last 20 years. History is not always clear on how poor the Black American was after being emancipated from slavery. (Source: U.S. Census Bureau, March 1995.)

## Lower Economic Middle Class Of Black Americans

These Black Americans earn approximately $11,000 to $19,000 as an income. This class of people may or may not have finished high school or may be fresh out of college. (Deduced from data from the National Urban League, 1996.)

## Upper Economic Middle Class Black Americans

About 17% of all Black households have incomes of $50,000-$80,000 or more as compared with 38% of all White American households. This class is growing as many Black Americans receive education and step out of the lower classes. Education is the first real full step to participate in the economic power of America. (Source: Two Nations: Black and White, separate, Hostile and Unequal by Andrew Hacker.) (Deduced from data from the National Urban League, 1996.)

## Upper Economic Class Black Americans

You can count the number of Black Americans who have managed to join this elite class of Americans, and they will be a force to reckon with in the near future. Most certainly, Oprah Winfry, Bill Cosby, Tiger Woods, and Michael Jordan would fit into this class. There are some Black American business names that you may not have ever heard of, such as Herman J. Russell of H.J. Russell & Company. H.J. Russell is a $165 million dollar (in revenue) construction conglomerate. Another is Earl Graves of the Graves Publishing Empire and publisher of Black Enterprise

Magazine and other Black Business publications, the source of much of the data in this book. Graves Publishing revenues are about $30 million a year. John H. Johnson of the Johnson Publishing Empire is another in this group. Johnson Publishing Empire includes Ebony and Jet Magazines, and makes about $325 million a year in sales. It was the first large Black-owned Company to sell Black personal care products. Robert L. Johnson, no relation to John H. Johnson, owns the Black Entertainment Television Network, popularly known as BET. BET's annual sales approach $135 million during the writing if this chapter. It was one of the first publicly offered Black-owned corporations on the New York Stock Exchange. Reginald Lewis, now deceased, of the Beatrice Corporation, was the first Black American to take-over a Fortune 500 corporation. TLC Beatrice is the largest grossing Black-owned Company in terms of gross sales, at $2.23 billion at the time of authorship. I am not sure how long we can still call it a Black-owned company. Loida Lewis, his wife, is running the firm and she is Asian, although his children, who are part Black, still own part of the company.

It is amazing what the White American does not know about the Black American. Black Americans are inundated with information on White America from all forms of media. Black Americans, whether they want to or not, are educated on the conditions of White America. On the other hand, Black American information is hard to find, even by a Black American who wishes to find it. The White American, who doesn't think of finding this sort of information about Black America, will not find it in the mainstream media. This is a tragedy for all Americans! We must know and understand each other if we are going to continue to be successful in a global economy. Being successful in a global economy is a goal all of us can agree upon – whether we are conservative republicans or liberal democrats or somewhere in between..

## *Are Black Americans Gaining Access To Capital In America?*

The answer here is yes. Black Americans have capital, and they are customers of the American banking system. This system, like all our other systems, has made much progress. But due to capitalistic competition, Black Americans, new players in this game, struggle to compete for the needed resources we call capital. We in America continue to live by discriminatory policies and practices that White American forefathers implemented years ago, without questioning them. Ironically, they designed these policies and practices with all great intentions, never realizing how much damage they would cause for hundreds of years. Because of this, Black American access to capital is much more limited than White Americans.

Our banking system grants people capital based on the assets they already have. If a person doesn't have any assets, he or she has no way to qualify to obtain the capital that is needed to get assets. That is why I always try to get young Black Americans to save money early in their lives. Once they have saved money, they can then purchase a home, which becomes their asset. I try to help them understand why they should start buying stocks in small amounts in order to build up equity, and, hence, assets that banks will use as collateral. Even as I write this paragraph, I am in the process of trying to borrow money to fund the publishing and marketing costs for this book. The task is a long and hard one. I have already been turned down by the large White commercial banks in the city where I live and conduct commerce. The officers of the banks want to help me, but the rules and regulations of the bank have determined that I am too high a risk to borrow their money. How do you fix these tough problems? One at a time!!!

At the time of this writing, I also pursued a loan through a community development bank. They are set up to help small, high-risk businesses such as mine; even they would not help me. There are only seven of these banks in the country. At this time, I hope they can accomplish the mission they were created to complete.

## *How Much Purchasing Power Do Blacks Have In America?*

A University of Georgia study found that Black American disposable income was $427 billion dollars.

A survey showed that Blacks had a personal buying power of $324 billion in 1995. Black American households out paced White American households in purchasing cars, children's clothing, and perishable foods. (Data source: Survey of 3000 Black American Households, Target Market News Inc., 1995, Chicago.)

Black Americans Purchased:

- $10.8 billion dollars in new cars
- $4.5 billion dollars worth of consumer electronics
- $697 million dollars worth of computer equipment
- $118 million dollars spent on sporting events
- $1.8 billion dollars spent on entertainment and leisure
- $4.2 billion dollars spent on travel and lodging

Target Market News conducts surveys to determine how Americans choose to spend their hard-earned cash, especially to identify consumer purchases. The survey also showed that Black American's purses were growing faster than all other segments of the population. Many Fortune 500 companies are starting to target Black Americans with products tailored for them.

## *Do Blacks Americans Understand The Financial Power They Have In America?*

You Bet! Too often this power is not understood when it comes to the personal finances of Black Americans. But, organizations like the Urban League, Rainbow Coalition, and the NAACP continue to educate Black Americans about the importance of wielding green power in America. I have talked about the Texaco debacle that happen as I was writing this book. After Texaco's upper management had been so blatantly stupid as to let themselves be taped during a meeting where they displayed racist behavior toward Black employees, Jessie Jackson called for a boycott of their products. Now, you must realize 31 million Black Americans in the U.S. spend $8.6 billion on gasoline alone. Texaco immediately felt the effect of this boycott from Black Americans. Add to that the White Americans that will not tolerate racial discrimination and supported the boycott, and Texaco received a clear message. Although they paid over $170 million to the Black employees who were party in this case, Texaco's image will continue to be tarnished for years to come.

Denny's felt the same powerful sting when Black FBI agents experienced racist behavior when they were refused service by Denny's staff. As I discussed in an earlier chapter, Denny's had to try for over three years to win back its customers. It ended up changing its CEO and significantly increasing the amount of minorities and women to its staff. The results have been an overall increase in their sales and profits. This is absolutely exciting to me. None of this would be effective if a significant part of the White American population hadn't joined in the public outcry over the abuse of their fellow Americans.

McDonald's Restaurants, on the other hand, has hired teams of consultants to learn how to capitalize on the Black American market. They know what kind of music they need to play behind their ads in order to entice Black Americans to buy their cheeseburgers. Their outstanding french-fries and the new hot apple pie taste as if they were made in my grandmother's oven 20 years ago. These are winners with the Black consumer. McDonald's has made the effort to understand Black Americans and to honor our dignity. It has proven to us, in a positive way, it wants our money. Although I like Wendy's food better, I am loyal to McDonald's for giving so many young Black American youths jobs after school.

One last example in this area is the sports apparel companies, with Nike leading the way. I see more Black Americans in the media, because Nike takes the time to understand how we buy things. Don't get me wrong, I am no fan of Phil Knight and company, but I do know he knows that Black Americans are important in selling and buying his products. Nike also understands something else that a lot of retailers don't, and that is how to use Black American money to make more White American money. Nike's latest product endorser is Tiger Woods. With Tiger's name, Nike will have more Black – and White – American golfers wearing Nike golf apparel. If this trend continues, Black Americans will certainly move closer to economic parity in America.

### Is Reparation A Solution To Enhance The Economic Outlook For Black Americans?

This is an old discussion that has recently resurfaced in the minds and mouths of Black academicians and economists. They do not see it as a single solution, but as a part of a package of solutions. This package might also include stopping race-based hatred and minimizing economic stress for Black Americans. Reparation would be a part of the solution for minimizing stress. This is too academic for me.

Giving Blacks money and land would help the Black economic condition, but that would be letting Mother America and Uncle Sam off the hook, far too easily. This country has far more responsibility to Black and White Americans than the 40 acres and a mule theory. In today's dollars that would equate to approximately $180,000 dollars per African American. I don't believe this will ever happen in my lifetime. Wealth and economic prosperity must be earned if they are to be sustained in a capitalistic society. Giving Black Americans, or any American, money without the economic education and experience to use it wisely is a waste of money. It doesn't help us compete in a society whose economy is founded on competition and the laws of supply and demand.

On the other hand, taking about ten billion dollars to reopen the education system would provide a tremendous win-win for all Americans. We must create a mind-set in America that is holistic and sustainable. This mind-set must include people envisioning how the whole of society can benefit from a prosperous Black America and, hence, a prosperous total America.

Reparation in the context of White and Black Americans agreeing on how to increase the economic opportunity of Black Americans will serve us all well. The "pay you back" theory because "I done you wrong," is obsolete at best. I have come to the understanding that America can only prepare to compete globally by working at the community level.

### *Does Sustainable Economic Development Hold Any Hope For Black Americans?*

Most Urban Cities are implementing Empowerment Zones and Sustainable Development in urban communities. Where do Black Americans fit in this scheme? Today that question is answered poorly.

In October of 1996, I had the opportunity to attend a very important conference. The Oregon Department of Economic Development conducted the conference for the Asian Pacific Economic Committee. The theme of the conference was "Sustainable Development, Networking and Information." I was very surprised to find my self in the midst of some very powerful Asian dignitaries and technological giants from all over the Pacific rim. The conference was well attended by the "who's who" of economic development from all over the United States. Corporate America was well represented as well. The conference had approximately 200 - 250 attendees. I was pleasantly frustrated when I found I was the only Black American at the conference. What I mean by pleasantly frustrated is that, I was glad to be there and sorry other Black Americans were not in attendance. On the third day of the conference when we went to our work session groups, I attended the work session on Sustainable Development for cities. When it was time for my input, I told the entire group that it was amazing to experience the exclusion of Black Americans in these all-important processes. Discussions about sustaining the environment or the economy are flawed if they don't address how to help all the participants of the society. What was very pleasing to me was the reactions of the White Americans in the group who came up to me and reassured me that I had surfaced an important issue. I knew that Black Americans were not intentionally omitted from this important process. Instead, the conference organizers had probably not thought that they were not including all Americans.

During the final main tent of the conference, I had the opportunity to ask a question of the Deputy Director of the Environmental Protection Agency. My question was what is the present administration doing to help urban centers become sustainable communities. He quickly did a three-minute dissertation on Empowerment Zones and Brown Field clean up. Brown Field cleanups are the hazardous waste sights in urban communities resulting from industry waste and landfills of yesteryears. Most of these sights are found right-smack-dab in the middle of Black communities. Most of the worst environmental sites were put in American ghettos, because the people did not understand how to fight the big companies or the government who were responsible for these hazards. I am glad to say the government is trying to do something about this serious problem.

I admit that many Black Americans do not get involved in complex issues such as these, because they do not understand the impact that these issues have on them and their economic well-being. There must be a concerted effort to bring opportunities to Black Americans and educate them as to why some of these issues are important to them. Most government agencies have large public outreach and involvement programs, but they are geared toward the highly-educated, more affluent Black Americans, who are already likely to protest if something threatens to adversely affect the community they call home.

By the way, the only reason I attended the conference was because my White American female colleague, who sits on a community economic development board with me, told me about the conference and recommended that I be invited to take her place since she was not able to attend. She has also been very good about letting me review some of the work she has done as a consultant on sustainable development for cities. I am deeply grateful to her for providing me the opportunity. (Thanks Pat Scruggs!)

## *Can Black Americans Only Improve Their Social-Economic Condition At The Detriment Of White Americans?*

This is one of the biggest myths in today's society. Black and White Americans equally share this odd ball way of thinking. This is one of the most damaging beliefs I have encountered in America. Most people believe if their neighbor's economic situation improves, they must be losing ground. The truth of the matter is America is doing so well that the entire economic pie continues to get bigger. The catch is, fewer and fewer Americans get a piece of that pie. If we can redirect our way of thinking to understand that America is a booming, rich, and thriving country and that will need of all its human capital in order to continue to have successful business commerce for all Americans. We would then start to value each other more. Our country was designed to be this way, and, although there are times when we might not like how we got here, here is a good place to be. Our economy was built by all of us and, therefore, it must be shared by all of us or we will destroy what we have created. That is what history has shown us over and over again.

On the other hand, America continues to experience economic growth, the fruits of doing the right things at the right time. That we would seek equity between Black and White Americans is inevitable. All of us stand to gain by promoting the economic well-being for all of America. If Black Americans don't continue to progress, they will move to the rolls of the unemployed, and will have to be sustained by tax dollars. White Americans stand to benefit a lot, if Black Americans continue to become a part of the sustaining force of the American economy. There are tremendous benefits for American society, if all our workforce is developing to leverage all of our resources, especially human resources. The key will be to continue making our human resources into human capital, which will then become the asset that can be copied, cloned, or matched by other countries, and will lead to a booming, thriving, successful World economy.

# Chapter
# 8

## Chapter Eight - Is There Really A "Black Thing" Whites Don't Understand?

We Blacks love to say the phrase "it's a Black thing," and often adding "you wouldn't understand." I must admit, we often use this phrase as away of excluding Whites from things we hold dear to our ethnicity. It is often our way of saying, "I really don't want to explain this to you, because it is not important to you." Most of the things we deem as Black things are nothing more than things we think give us our ethnic make-up, and many of them are created in current day America. They don't come from Africa, nor were they passed down through our African heritage. The ability to create them in the way we do may be due to cultural heritage, but few are exclusively Black.

I will share with you a little secret, if you truly and genuinely demonstrate your interest in knowing one of these things, you will probably get more information than you originally wanted from most of us Black folk. A word of caution: do not push too hard if it is one of those protected and sacred Black things we truly do not want to share with you. For instance, many Blacks call each other "my nigger." This is very sacred communication and any White person who has risen to this level of trust with a Black person has far exceeded American cultural expectations for Black and White relationships. I have never had a White friend to this day whom I have allowed to call me a nigger; it's a Black Thing. Some have tried, and I have shut them down very quickly. Many of my White friends have become very dear to me over the years, and I have learned to cherish their friendships, but none have yet risen to this level of trust. They had not come close to earning that privilege, and I don't think any of my White friends ever will. Personally, I don't like this particular Black thing and I don't allow many of Black friends to use the term in my presence.

The Black dialect is a sacred Black thing, although I am glad to see White Americans learning to communicate using Black slang and idioms or what use to be considered ghetto talk. There is a noted White talk show host in the Portland, Oregon area that is very eloquent in the universal Black dialect. The neat thing about this particular talk show host is her ability to use the dialect throughout the program, and she doesn't have many Black callers (unless she is dealing with a Black interest topic.) She does a part of the news, and often converses with high-level government officials and corporate managers. She loves to say, "Wuts Up?" in Black dialect. She does speak the typical English of the media, however, when she is dealing with a serious issue.

When Whites use Black slang and idioms, we Blacks really would like them to earn that privilege. A part of being Black is sharing privileges that are given to you, because you are Black. I am not sure where this talk show host learned the dialect, and I don't know how she got so comfortable using the Black dialect, but she is. She may have dated a Black guy or had a Black girlfriend in college. If any of those experiences were afforded her she has earned the privilege. She now has to be careful on how, when and where she takes her liberties. From my observations and estimation, she has been very eloquent in her usage of the Black dialect.

Another Black Thing is the ability of Black people to communicate with each other without ever saying a word. We are often guilty of using too many words when talking to each other. If we are in the company of many Whites and there are only a few of us, we can give an encouraging look that says, I see you my sister and I am glad you are here. Whites might do the same thing when they are in a foreign country where they are now in the minority, like one of the African countries. They see another White person and they acknowledge them without speaking words. Usually, they will try to talk to each other. When I was in the military,

I had the opportunity to visit several foreign countries. There was an amazing "American thing" at work. It didn't matter whether we were Black, White, Asian, or whatever, if we saw the American uniform, we acknowledged each other. The example shows that Blacks have no corner on the market for having things they hold dear to their culture. The Irish Americans have their things. The German Americans have their things. The unfortunate result of the assimilation process is that it wipes out these "things."

Blacks struggle to hold on to these things, because the assimilation process makes it easy to give them up. One Black thing that is not often recognized by Whites as a Black thing is our hairstyles. This is our way of expressing our ethnicity. Whites are starting to realize how important it is to us. I do like the way young White youth is latching on to some of these styles with some modifications, due to the texture of White hair. They need to express themselves, as well. If we give up our hairstyles and take on Euro-American hairstyles, which, according to the media, are defined by Clairol, Covergirl or the Hair Club For Men (for us baby boomers), we are seen as strange.

For a long time our hair was called nappy instead of tightly curled, and it was considered unattractive by White America, who as I stated earlier, define what is accepted by American culture, including for Black people. We Blacks have attempted to assimilate our hairstyles. The conk was our first attempt, as demonstrated by Denzel Washington and Spike Lee in the biography of Malcolm X. The conk was a harsh process and often left burns on the scalp. The gericurl was our recent day attempt to assimilate more into the mainstream American culture. For those of you who don't know what a gericurl is, it is a process of relaxing the tight curl of Black hair. Michael Jackson sported a gericurl during his "Thriller Video Era." Today, most Blacks see the gericurl as rejecting the beauty of natural Black hair, and I agree. I have never worn a gericurl and never wanted one. Natural Black hair has become one of those Black things that we have learned to like about ourselves. America has accepted the natural style of Black hair, which I think, is good. We are the only race with truly curly hair, when untreated by chemicals. A note of interest: Whites often think they are being complimentary when they say they wish their hair wasn't so straight or had more curl. Blacks often feel patronized or mocked during these times of trust building. If you do have an exchange of this sort, make sure the person you are talking to know you are sincere.

One Black Thing that has become a part of the American culture is the Black Power handshake. I now see many Whites using it, not only with Black people, but also with each other. This level of usage shows it has become a part of the American culture. However, it is still very sacred to Blacks. For a while we attempted to complicate it to frustrate Whites from learning it. I believe it got too complicated for us as well, and we have reverted to the simpler version.

### What Is Truly Important To The Black American Of Today?

Understanding the answer to this question could move Black and White relationships ahead by light years. As I shared earlier, Black Americans have been forced to understand a lot about White Americans. They have been assimilating into the American culture for sometime, a culture that is very White and American. If White Americans would take a break from solving problems to learn what is truly important to Black America, they would find that we share a tremendous amount of the same values and societal mores. We care about America, each other and you.

First and foremost Black Americans want to be valued by their country. They want to be recognized as a contributing member to the community and to their neighbors. Black Americans helped build this country from the time this land was first settled by non-Native Americans. We fought in every war that has ever been fought in this land, since we arrived 300 plus years ago. We have always had the highest per capita participation in all the wars and in all the deaths that America has fought. Did you know more than 300,000 Black Americans died during the Civil War? I would call that highly participative. Yes, I am the first to admit the reason I joined the navy was to get out of the ghetto, but isn't a part of the American Dream to be able to take advantage of the opportunities offered by this great country?

Second, they want to receive the benefits that every other taxpayer in America receives, and don't want to depend on the welfare system any more than other Americans do. Since we started welfare reform, young Black female welfare recipients have been getting off the rolls of welfare, going to more job fairs, and becoming a part of the working society. The opportunity to work is one of the most exhilarating feelings one could have. We Black Americans treasure and value the opportunity as much as our White counterparts.

Third, we want a good education for our children and the opportunities that follow that education. These opportunities are often illusive for Black Americans, even after we achieve the all-important American indoctrination. I remember being in college and how vibrant I felt when I was studying and learning. It is only through education that we start to solve some of our complex race relations-problems in America.

Fourth, we want to own a piece of the rock. Most Americans don't realize how complicated it can be to own a piece of the rock. Learning how to work in the real estate and financial systems of America are very complicated processes. Many Black Americans never come close to understanding how it works. I also know a lot of White Americans find our financial institution very complicated, particularly the process of financing or capitalizing a project. To effectively use this tool of capitalism is required to be successful in America.

Fifth, Black Americans seek the same self-actualization that White Americans seek: learning, opportunity, and – if you haven't latched on to it yet – participation. I realized this when I finally built my family's house on a hill, had a nice car and a place at the beach, then realized it was not enough. I had a great desire to own a business. I have risked everything to make my business go forward, and I am learning a lot about being an American who has experienced failure.

Sixth, Black Americans must be allowed to fail. One Black American failing does not mean all Black Americans have failed. I have personally learned that failure leads to success, and without it all you have is luck. Luck is too unpredictable and undependable. Failure is necessary, if we are to learn to succeed. I have a lot of White friends who have failed and tried again and failed again. If they keep trying in America, they will eventually succeed. Look at Mr. Bill Gates, a genius, but also a social failure. He has yet to finish his education. In the American society he has failed, but we all know that is a joke!

Finally, at least for now, dignity is important to all human beings and our existence. If we have no sense of our own worth and who we are, we will use a tactic that even the Borg would never use, and that is to destroy what we have. Being a part of a group that has a collective set of values and goals that all members work to meet is a tremendous binding agent. Young kids have a natural propensity to play with each other, but the process of making this happen is not always easy. First, they struggle with possession and ownership over their toys and territory. Then, they have to know how they will benefit from the situation. But, where kids excel over us adults is their ability to remove the obstacles and rapidly overcome differences. I believe they go through the same set of checks and balances, but with less fear and complexity. They are willing to take risk in their building of relationships.

Black Americans very badly want to be completely accepted by America. They have learned to value what they have, and they are not willing to forfeit what they were forced to in the past. They know that another chapter in history is being written, and it will be different than the last one. And, they fully understand they are now one of the writers that must be allowed to participate.

*Are There Unique Black American Practices?*

There are many practices that we Black Americans hold dear, and these practices are often misread as barriers by those who don't understand them. I will attempt to share a few of them in the next few sections to help you gain a better understanding of them. Once you understand them, you may find yourself using them with your Black friends or colleagues. Don't be afraid to experiment when learning how to use them. You may appear a little silly trying to use them before you master them, but think of how Japanese feel when they are trying to learn things within the American culture. I find it fascinating to learn something about another culture and, if I can participate, I am tickled to death, as the saying goes, to be made a part of the learning.

**Do Blacks Americans Like To Rename Themselves?**

There is a practice in the Black community of giving each other nicknames. There are folk tales that this was done because the slaves did not like the names that were given to them by their masters. I have not seen any historical references to prove or disprove this notion. The movie "Roots" portrayed the slaves as not willing to give up their African names, and I believe that to be true. There is a wonderful cultural practice in the Black communities of America of Black folks giving each other nicknames that are usually accepted as terms of endearment. My mother called me Darrell Deannie, and most of the kids in my neighborhood and schools called me Deano. My brother still calls me Deano and I call him Poochie (his real name is Melvin, after my father). His wife doesn't like this nickname. She always tell us her husband is not a dog. Another one of my brothers lost his front tooth when we were kids, and we all nickname him "Snag" as in Snaggletooth, a cartoon character from our childhood. My brother's real name is Gregory, but I occasionally still call him Snag.

One of my cousins was very good at football and I had the opportunity to practice against him when we tried out for little league football. During the practice he was running with the ball, and I attempted to tackle him. He kept running and bucking like a horse and hit me with his helmet. I still have the scar to prove it. We nicknamed him "Buck." His real name is Ronald. I have another cousin who ran one of the fastest legs of our high school all district 440-relay team. He has bowlegs, which may have helped his speed, but made him attractive to the girls in our school. He always had a cute girlfriend during our high school years. We nicknamed him "Billy Hooks," his real name is Willard. We called his brother Snow and he inherited this name from their father. Their real name was Noel. This is the uncle I discuss in a later chapter, who had two households.

This practice was also true for the females in our family and community. We had one girl in our neighborhood that acted like a spoil brat, and we aptly nicknamed her "Spoily." I cannot even remember her real name. We often shorten many girls' names. Joan Marie was called "John," yes, just like John F. Kennedy. My sister Cynthia was called "Cynt." My sister Patricia was called "Pat," and my sister Majesta was called, "MA." A celebrity, I introduced in an earlier chapter, Florence Griffith Joyner, was affectionately nicknamed "Flo-Jo."

Many Black Americans who grew up in the south are called by their first and middle name. There are names like "Betty Sue" and "Doris Ann." I have found this also practiced by southern White Americans. There are names like "Billy Joe" and "Sally Mae." You may be able to think of a few others.

Nicknames are something we enjoy creating and using. Even today, I find myself shortening people's names or using their initials, which is another part of the nicknaming practice. There were a lot of R.J.s around my neighborhood. In the professional world, I call most of my White colleagues by their initials, which they accept without complaint. My favorite administrative assistant of all times is Susan, whom I call "Suz." What is neat about how we have developed our working relationship and friendship, she reciprocates and calls me just plain "D." Neat huh? All of my staff picked up on it. I like it; it makes me feel accepted and included in their circle.

Some final notes on these so-called "Black Things." These so-called "Black Things" are nothing more than practices and activities that continue to define who Black people are in America. Remember the majority of our role models look like you. We do not like to admit this all-important fact, but it is true. We fight having you as role models in many ways, because for many years Black Americans were not allowed to emulate White Americans without grave consequences. When a people has been kept from developing through a normal process, such as assimilating into America, the damage is long-lasting and takes a long time to repair. As an optimist and an American, you will continue to hear me say, I believe anything can be repaired with the appropriate amount of time and money.

# Chapter
# 9

## Chapter Nine - Are All Black Americans Angry At The World?

*T*here is deep-seated anger in the Black American people. Although some Black people would disagree, after they read this chapter I believe they would agree with many points. Remember this is one person's perspective on a very emotional topic. I should begin by saying I am angry with America, because it has not solved the racial problems that resulted from a long historic struggle and process. This struggle is the tension of Black and other Americans trying to participate in the opportunities afforded by this land. The process, again, is the assimilation process and all its distinctive selectivity elements and components. I understand that the American of today, Black or White, struggles with how to fix these problems. None of us were here when it started, and we don't understand how we got to this point. Although we don't agree on a solution, most Americans would like to see racial conflict and strife go away.

Many American resources are spent trying to rectify situations around the world, but not enough time is spent on problems on our own shores. Often, we are like little children; we hear a noise on the other side of the fence, and have to find out what is going on over there. Once we go and look, then we want to see more of what is happening over there. If we think there is a chance that we will lose something because of what is happening on the other side of the fence, we are enticed to go over there to understand what the commotion is about. We forget what is going on in our own back yard. We simply jump the fence to get to the other side, without regard to what we are getting into.

Before we know it, we find ourselves deeply involved in someone else's problem. We are good at getting involved in other people's problems; it is a huge past time for our government. I am angry to see us force our resources on people who do not even want them, while neglecting our own problems.

This anger should not to be confused with the anger you display when you disagree with someone over a political matter or sports issue. It should also not be confused with an angry reaction to someone who has wronged you. In my last book, I named this anger the "Black Chip." It's an anger that is embedded in Black Americans' deepest and most protected areas of our hearts and souls. This anger gives Black people "the ability to turn back the clock to a time of pure hell and oppression." The Black Chip has a significant historical basis, traceable to how our ancestors were treated. You are right to think that this anger is primarily counterproductive and should be released. I agree. I have spent my entire life trying to let go of this anger.

I left my hometown of New Orleans after concluding that this anger was too pervasive in my hometown and often misdirected. This anger was all consuming and can overwhelm the very elite of the Black people of America. I discovered it is destructive to my friends and families. Some of my friends gave into the dark side of this anger, letting it develop into hate for the system and for themselves. Many of the kids I grew up with were consumed by this anger; they are no longer alive today. Because of this anger, one of my brothers is in a penal institution in the bowels of New Orleans. It hurts my heart to know that society failed him and even me for a time. It failed him in that he will spend most of his youth in an institution that will not make him any better than when they first incarcerated him. It failed me when I realized I needed to run away from New Orleans to survive. I now realize that I was running from the same net that ensnared him. But I escaped.

I have another brother (Snag) who was also caught in the same net, but at a much younger age. I am glad he squirmed out through a hole called education. He was a very angry kid when he was young. Somehow, he found himself and radically changed the direction in which he was headed. He not only finished high school; he also finished college and is now a successful commercial photographer in New Orleans. I would like to think that he used me as a role model to spur him on to success. He is very involved in his church and that has helped him over come some great personal challenges. He has now become my role model and inspiration, because of his approach to life and business. He smiles a lot these days.

Even today this anger tears at the core of a significant portion of Black American youth. Too many kids will end up like my younger brother and they won't make it out. Most of the rap music written by young Black Americans describes what they don't have or what they can't get. Many Black American youth are consumed with the idea that they are going nowhere and gaining nothing from this life, they will then turn to very destructive survival schemes.

This anger doesn't often manifest itself obviously. The individuals don't get involved in riots and physical destruction until they have been overwhelmed with anger. The Black Chip lies so deep that you might say it's "spiritually" deep. Earlier I mentioned that I was angry. But I hardly ever seem angry – I'm a happy and enthusiastic person who loves life. I'm a typical middle-class American, who cares about family, friends, community, politics and society as a whole. Please do not misunderstand the definition of this anger. If anything, try to understand where it originated, and how it plays out in the society of today.

The anger you see in Black Americans is an evolving anger. It is often an internally destructive anger. If allowed to evolve to its fullest, it expresses itself as hatred and even violence against White Americans. Too often this anger is misdirected. One very bad side affect is that it is often focused intraculturally. An example of this intracultural focus is Black on Black crime or Blacks rioting in their own communities. In the western part of the United States it is creating crises in our communities. This anger, born out of frustration, can be misread as stupidity. Remember what you learned in your Psychology 101 class. Thoughts based on strong emotions usually erupt into action. This anger can also have an intercultural focus, by aiming at a culture that appears to be getting a better break in America than Black Americans.

The Korean community has faced this anger during the Rodney King Riots in Los Angeles. Black Americans destroyed and looted Korean stores that had moved into the Black community during more peaceful times. Black Americans in LA observed what they thought to be injustice on the part of Rodney King, and exploded against the Korean Community and all other cultures they thought had earlier invaded their communities. With all due respect to other ethnic Americans, such as the Asian and Hispanic communities, they often ride the crest that has been created by the progressive struggles of Black Americans. Struggles that have led to many positive changes to the American system for people of color. This, in turn, frustrates Black Americans even more.

These intercultural explosions result from pressure that has been building in our communities for years. I don't profess to be a sociologist, anthropologist or psychologist, but from experience I know that if you observe and think through some of these events you can gain valuable insights into any culture's thinking process. If many of us gain these insights and improve our understanding, we may create wonderful solutions to our racial problems in America.

This anger is important to understand if you want to tear down the walls of enmity that exist between White and Black America. If you want to understand how to build solid relationships between Black and White people, you should understand how this anger works. Not understanding how this anger works leads to pushing the wrong cultural buttons and getting bad results. America does this on a regular basis to Black Americans. Sometimes Black Americans do this to themselves. This is not done intentionally, as some paranoid Black Americans have come to believe. For instance, many Blacks believe that the AIDS virus was released to exterminate Blacks. If that was the plan, it backfired on White, and all other, Americans. Even if there was one White American who came up with this crazy plan, I could never let that notion overshadow how I feel about all White Americans. I simply believe that this sort of thinking on the part some Black Americans continues to fan this "anger." Regardless of how these notions come about, they only end up pushing cultural buttons.

There is another example of how America pushes the wrong buttons for Black Americans. I was very angry on the day of this writing after hearing about a story that broke in San Jose, California. The headline read, "CIA linked to flood of cocaine to L.A. gangs." The story explained how court records and a newspaper investigation tied U.S. Run Contra guerrillas to Los Angeles gangs. Yes, I did say the United States was controlling Latin American armies. Get this, the funding for these contra guerrillas was coming from drugs sold directly into Los Angeles, specifically, Black communities in south central Los Angeles. The money that flowed through those communities perpetuated the violence those communities were already experiencing – violence that is connected to the low social economic status of those communities. I became even angrier when I read about the devastation that these communities will continue to bear from the many homeless crack addicts. Thousands of young Black men will continue to serve sentences for selling the cocaine. Cocaine was never seen in these neighborhoods before the CIA's army brought dope into them. We are talking about the U.S. government trying to bring about democracy in another country while it allows that country to sell drugs to the Black American community. You bet I get angry when the country I love is assisting in the destruction of my children. This even makes me paranoid! The end does not justify the means, as was stated by a Nicaraguan Democratic Force (FDN) member during a trial. He said that the CIA agent who was in command of the FDN told him this story. Bringing this type of destruction to a people results in deep-seated anger that, in turn, leads to destructive hatred. Oh! All this information appeared in the San Jose Mercury News as reported by Gary Webb, an investigative reporter. USA Today broadcasted it nationally.

Too often anger that was born in our history re-surfaces when some angry White person burns a cross on a lawn to make a statement about how he or she feels about Black people. I believe that White people who work up the courage to burn a cross on some Black person's lawn are not a true racist; they are probably as disenchanted with society as the Black people they set out to harass. In America, it is hard for someone to come to the point of hating an entire race of people. But someone who wants a place to vent anger can associate their anger with an entire group of people who share a distinguishing physical attribute, such as skin color. Black people are often the target of anger that is created from society's ill wills or tensions. For example, society targets all Black people for abusing the welfare system and is disenchanted with all Black men for not being good fathers.

Question:What people have the highest divorce rate in the world? Answer: White Americans. White fathers don't come under the same scrutiny as Black fathers. The difference is that the courts know how to make a working White father pay his child support. America feels good about a man who owns up to his family financial responsibility. Black men have the highest unemployment rate in the nation. Black men leave families, because they lose all hope for taking care of their families. They are poorly educated and have little opportunity to get a job to support their families. They leave their families knowing they can rely on the welfare system. Please don't think I am letting them off the hook; I am trying to give you a perspective. Check this story out about my Uncle Noel (Snow) I mentioned in the last chapter.

I had an uncle who I thought was married to my aunt. They had four children. My uncle was a longshoreman, and was a very good provider for his family. Later in life, I found out my uncle was not married to my aunt, but was actually married to another woman who had several children with him. He lived with this other woman when he wasn't with my aunt. He cared for that family as well as he cared for my aunt and her children. For many years, he took care of my family when my mother needed help. He cared for both these families for many years. The two families barely lived two miles apart. He ran both households, and raised all the children very well. I later found out that my aunt and the other woman knew each other well, as a matter of fact, I heard my aunt refer to the woman many times when chiding my uncle. No, I don't condone him for having two wives, but he most certainly met his responsibilities. Just an interesting side story with an interesting twist. End Digression

Americans believe the stereotype that Black men don't care for their families, and this fuels the anger within us. I continue to challenge Black people to find the positive side of everything. I must admit it does not take much to get Black people very upset over the way they have been treated in America. For more information, refer back to "Has Every Black American Had A Bad Experience" – Chapter Six.

This Black anger has a current basis as well. America continues to tell us that we now have every opportunity that a White American has, but we continue to see Black Americans face many inequities. Black people want to go out and scream at the world, stop lying to me — stop treating me as if I am stupid. Stop telling me everything is okay, then turn around and exclude me from basic things that America offers.

Imagine being a young Black woman, fresh out of engineering school. Your mother, father, aunts, and uncles have told you, girl, go to school, study hard, and you will be successful. Now here you are with degree in hand and, for two years, you can't find a job. Every one of the white engineers who graduated with you got a job within six months of graduating. Many of them were second generation and, because of nepotism, were placed in small engineering firms. During your two-year search you build a network of friends that reaches into City Hall. That network finally leads you to another Black inside a large engineering firm that does a large amount of the design work to fix the infrastructure in America. The firm hires you, because of affirmative action. The firm is predominantly white and male, as are most large engineering design firms in America. But that doesn't bother you, you got used to being the only Black female engineer while you were in college. You are overjoyed to finally have the chance to use the degree that everyone had said would pay off. Now you think that they were right.

The first few months you feel good. Everyone introduces him or herself to you, and welcomes you to the firm. About the fourth month, you boss tells you there is not much work to do. You don't understand, because you see everyone very busy and always complaining they have too much work to do. Several people give you work to do, which you finish, and you start to look for more. You start to realize they are all fairly good at doing certain parts of the engineering design. Your boss tells you not to worry; he will find work for you. He comes to you a day later, asking you to update the equipment specification manuals. This is the most boring work you have ever experienced, but, being the trooper, you give it all you got. Each day you go home drained because of the monotonous routine of opening three-ring binders, removing pages, and replacing them with the more up-to-date ones. You find out from one of your colleagues that you are doing work that the administrative staff has postponed because of its workload. You now start to think, everyone has to pay his or her dues, but that does not seem to help how you feel. All the other young engineers seem to be enthused with their work. Your boss drops a hint that most of the engineers in the department have a masters degree. You get a cold feeling inside. You had the feeling before when they told you your grades were too low to finish engineering school but you graduated with a BS in civil engineering. You find yourself bounced around from project to project, assisting other engineers with mundane tasks that they don't want to do. You finally realize this is not getting any better and then one day you do not want to go back to work. Your self-esteem goes in to the toilet, and you are very depressed.

I watched this happen to a young woman not long ago. It is easy to let anger grow when you are faced with these scenarios in life. She actually handled the situation very well. If this happened to a young White woman the results would likely be the same.

But, this happens too often to young Black people. Yes, they get these opportunities based on affirmative action hires, and, if it were not for affirmative action, those firms would continue to grow more and more white and male.

## *Is There Any Productive Use Of All The Energy Generated By This Anger?*

Don't ever forget how nations are built. The driving force is usually conflict, and conflict leads to violent, lengthy confrontations known as wars. I am not a subscriber of growth through pain and suffering, but I do know that it has been an effective agent in our history. I hope and pray that we skip this step in our quest to eradicate the enmity between the races in this country. We have to be very committed to removing racism from this land if all of us are going to take up the quest to make this country a better place for all Americans.

In spite of the negative consequences of this anger, Black Americans use this anger in a positive way all the time. It is at least one of the motivating factors for writing this book. If one gets sick and tired of the way one is positioned in society then it is time to change what one is doing. Yea right! Every time I see one of those movies on T.V. about racial injustice of the 50's and 60's, I am motivated to teach America a new way. A better way! It is my anger that drives me to love this country more. I believe my forefathers worked hard to make this a great nation, and I should have an opportunity to enjoy it. I refuse to be denied my privilege of being a proud American. Every time I am reminded that I don't have full access to all resources and systems of this great country, I get angry. I will keep trying! (He said with a smile!)

# Chapter
# 10

## Chapter Ten - What Affect Does the Media Have on Black and White American Relations?

 Who is the true conveyor of information, and who is the true teacher of those of the American way of life? Before I went to college, I didn't read newspapers, listen to all-news radio stations, or watch news programs such as "Nightline," "CNBC", "48 Hours," or "20-20." After attending a class at the University about the media, I became fascinated by the power of the media. It was one of the most popular elective classes among students of every academic field. Most students, including me, tried to take it in their sophomore year. The professor was a tremendously powerful speaker; I couldn't wait to hear what he had to say next.

What fascinated me were the various forms of the media, and how pervasive they are by informing the public in many ways, times, and places. The newspaper, which is read by most Americans during breakfast, still has me under its spell. I am addicted to reading the paper, and I get upset if something interferes with the time I set aside to partake in this daily ritual! It amazes me how many corporate business heads start their day by reading the Wall Street Journal or the newest national paper, USA Today. USA Today is delivered to the front door to more American business travelers than even its preppy precursor, The Wall Street Journal.

Then, there is Newsweek, Fortune, and U.S. News magazines. These magazines continue to increase their distribution, and editors of these so-called "trade rags" claim readership of three times as many people as those who actually purchase them. I know I read one of these whenever I am waiting in a reception area and one is available. I admit there are some magazines I refuse to read, like The National Enquirer or The Star.

Electronic media, such as radio or television, has extremely powerful message creation and distribution. If I am in the car, I immediately turn on the radio to get the latest news update. In this regard, I don't think I am much different than most educated Americans who listen to the radio on the way to the office and on the way home. With the advent of the Walkman radio, people now listen to the radio while riding the bus or other commuter services. (They also read the newspaper while commuting.)

After observing my children during the summer months, I am convinced that aliens have put television here and they are slowly absorbing all of our children's attention. My 17-year-old daughter will sit in front of the television from the time she gets up in the morning until she lays her head on her pillow at night. She is totally mesmerized by everything that the one-eyed monster presents. Just about every movie made is available on video. I admit, I am personally addicted to the VCR, and whenever a new action video is released, I must see it with my friend John. His wife, the editor of this book, calls it male bonding.

I am afraid of the way that the Internet provides information, especially sensational information. Our future is going to be filled with new devices that will continue to overload us with information, and a lot of that information is not going to be positive. All of these sources together make up a very powerful resource that gets used for us and against us. We continue to build this all-knowing, all-powerful thing we call the **MEDIA**.

The media is much more powerful than we think, especially when it comes down to shaping our thinking about each other. Dr. Marilyn Kern-Foxworthy, a Texas A&M University professor who studies child development, states that by the time a person reaches 18, he or she has watched 356,000 television commercials and public service announcements. Nielsen television rating studies have revealed that Black households watch about 72 hours of TV per week, about 49% more than households in any other groups do. McDonalds and Burger King are certainly aware of these statistics.

I don't think there is any debate about who controls most of the television programming in America; it is White America. By controlling what information goes into the public's head, this group can control what the public thinks about. I do not want you to believe, or think that I believe, that White Americans have some great think tank doing research or brainstorming on how to control what Americans are thinking about each other. I do not believe that the average White American spends a significant amount of time trying to figure out how to make it hard for Black Americans. I refuse to believe anything of the sort. I do believe there are by-products of the media that adversely affect Blacks in America.

As I stated earlier, I am a media freak, or maybe I should clarify that – I am a movie freak! Anybody that puts a good action script to film has my attention. With the advent of the VCR, I have found my one true thrill. I love to watch movies, and I have made a significant investment in the technology. I have a complete section of my house devoted to my favorite past time, watching movies. My goal is to own one thousand videos. I am also an information culturalist. This is simply a person who believes this is the information age, and likes to get as much information as he or she can absorb on topics of interest. As I said earlier, I read the paper in the morning and listen to the radio, mainly the news, on the way to work. I listen to the radio on the way home and finish the newspaper at the dinner table. And when Friday comes, I am at Captain Video, a video rental store. But, I have a love-hate relation with the media. It is the media that continues to perpetuate society's tendency to think of people as stereotypes.

By letting the media shape stereotypes of people, our society has ended up with some very interesting results. Let me quickly and clearly get this on the table: Black people are as good at stereotypic thinking as any other people. We also consume and regurgitate information that flows our way each and everyday. As a matter of fact, I find Black people stereotype themselves more than White people when it comes to the "have's" and the "have-not's." A lot of Blacks who have had success in America are very critical of Blacks who have not reached the American Dream. I often catch myself scrutinizing my fellow Black fathers to see if they are performing their duties as fathers. I quickly criticize anyone whom I believe is not doing his part. I realize I can be judgmental. Where do I base the information for making these conclusions? The media! It is hard to live in America and not believe that Blacks do a poor job parenting their children. The fact of the matter is, Black parents work harder than White parents at making sure their children are cared for. You may not agree with some of the methods used, including a Black father leaving home if he cannot support his family. Many do this to allow the rest of the family to get government assistance. They don't leave their families to shirk their duties, but because they feel hopelessness and despair at not being able to adequately provide for their family. The media portrays this as Black men sowing wild oats, leaving their children for you and me to care for. The reason why you find Black women losing their benefits after having more children is because their husbands return to the family to provide and supplement government support. In these cases, Black fathers are trying to fully support their families, but end up fathering more children.

### What Are Stereotypes?

As discussed in the preceding section, the media is powerful at perpetuating stereotypes. What, exactly, is a stereotype? Stereotypes are used to classify people, places, and things. Stereotypes are commonly used to distinguish people who are different from us: an entire race, class of people, and a gender. Too often stereotypes are used to divide White and Black Americans. The media uses stereotypes to fuel sensationalism every chance possible.

Stereotypes are so much embedded into our thinking processes that we use them unconsciously. If you are driving a car and another car moves in front of you too close for comfort, what is your first thought? It's some old woman who shouldn't be driving. But if you later see that the person is not an old woman, you may think that the driver must be a young woman who just got her license. With a second glance you may see the driver has short hair, so you surmise, this must be a teenager. You continue to affirm or modify stereotypes as you get more information.

A more commonplace example of stereotyping is this example. Imagine that a White woman parks her car in a shopping mall parking lot, and walks toward the mall. As she's walking, she notices two young teenage Black youths walking toward her. She looks and doesn't see anyone else around. Her reaction is to clutch her purse more tightly and put her arm through the purse strap. The Black youth continue to walk toward her, and her heart rate increases. The youth look at her and smile as they walk past her. But they snicker as they notice her switch the purse to be farther away from them. By the time Black people are 15 years old, they are no longer surprised by this behavior; this scenario is that common. But we never get used to having someone afraid of us, because of the color of our skin. If you were a Black person, you would probably have experienced this phenomenon before you were twelve. I'd almost guarantee it.

The following is an example of how devastating the misuse of stereotypes can be. Imagine a young White woman walking home from school is stopped by a Black man who beats her and takes her money. She alone has a valid reason to be scared of that Black man. The media reports this story to the public, adding sensationalism by showing a sketch that depicts this man in an unflattering manner. If the media uncovers negative facts about the man, they will report them. A good reporter will do this effectively, as there are incentives to make this story as sensational as possible. As a result every woman who reads or sees this story is afraid of all Black men. Some may argue that the media helps make the world safer by reporting stories in this way. But I believe they continue to divide Americans based on the stereotypes that they have perpetuated. The facts are that only one Black man violated one White woman. But, the entire Black male race will pay for it forever. This particular stereotype is generally accepted that Black men hurt and rob White women. In fact, this stereotype has been perpetuated further, so that all women, including Black women, are afraid of Black men.

If a young White man had accosted the White woman, she may have run home to her father and brother, and felt safe minutes after her father put his arms around her. She would have described this incident as "a man hurt me and stole my money." Note that she doesn't mention race. But, if a Black man hurt her, she probably would have specified race, as in "a Black man hurt me and took my money." In fact she may even describe the incident as "a big black nigger took my money and hurt me." Note how this negative stereotype transformed the effect of one incident to an entire group of people. The result of this can be vicious and cruel. And we have to live with this cruelty every day.

The only way for the media to change these negative experiences is to overwrite them with many, many positive experiences and examples. Instead, the media broadcasts to every reader and viewer how Black men hurt people; this message is drilled in over and over. Am I being unfair to the media, or has this been your experience as well?

### Can The Media Be Objective?

Even when the media is being objective, it continues to divide Americans based on the color of our skin. All media is guilty. I don't advocate restricting the media's right to free speech, which is important in informing and entertaining us. But it should be more careful how it reports. Although I have received great media coverage when I wrote my first book and was involved with the community, I am still tough on what the media considers objective coverage.

Americans need the media to work for us as much as it has worked against us. It has tremendous power to educate, and I hope it continues in that role. It is the best tool and methodology we have for breaking down the same stereotypic thinking it helps to perpetuate. I recognize the media does not intentionally set out to inflict the damage it creates. Most reporters just want to do a good job, have their stories on the front page or in the evening news. In fact, I wouldn't mind it if I achieved that with this book!

### What Affect Does Television Have On The Black/White Relationship?

Up until the mid 80's when Bill Cosby was depicted as an upstanding father without any quirky hang ups, Blacks had no real model of a successful Black family on television. All the good families were the White families. Bill Cosby was surrounded with shows like Family Ties, Too Close for Comfort, and Roseanne. O.J. Simpson was still running through airports and could do no wrong for Hertz rental cars. They were both great role models for men like myself.

But the media has pulverized both these men, perhaps rightly so. The media's biggest news story of the nineties was the O.J. Simpson trial. The media frenzy will go down in history as one of the most profound media blitzes of the 90's. O.J. is no longer the good-looking, high-stepping, record-breaking football star of the 80's. He is now the murderer, woman-abuser, and poor father of the century who murdered a white man and woman. I am not saying the media was wrong for covering this story, or even how they covered this story. I am saying it, again, has affected the way White and Black Americans view each other. Around 1997, Bill Cosby went through a court case that left him tainted as a man who was, at the least, unfaithful to his wife. I am not proud of either of these men, and the media definitely influenced me in reaching these conclusions.

In a similar vein, the media continues to depict the lifestyles of the rich and famous. Most of the Rich and Famous Blacks you see are athletes, entertainers, or singers. Here is one place where the media could help America by showing some of the prominent Black American business people I mentioned in an earlier chapter. Give America a look at how I. Barry Rand has progressed in his career at Xerox. Tell about the twenty Black professional women who have top positions in corporate America, as presented in Black Enterprise Magazine every year, and how they control over $36 billion of revenues and budgets. Great examples include Ann Fudge, the Executive Vice President of Kraft Foods and General Manager of the Maxwell House Coffee Division. Another example is Glenda Goodley McNeal, who is Vice President of American Express. There are lots of Black Americans who can satisfy the need of the American media for sensationalism and still present a positive message to America.

### What Does The Media Say Is Perfection?

The media continues to instruct us in portraying the good and bad in American culture. One serious problem this creates for Americans is that we let the media define what is good and perfect in America for us. If you have not seen the movie Malcolm X, starring Denzel Washington and Spike Lee, you should. It will help you get the most out this discussion. There is one tremendous scene where Malcolm is in prison and is being taught by a Muslim minister. The minister shows Malcolm how indoctrinated he has become to the White man's world. The minister points out the difference between Black and White according to the definitions in the dictionary. Webster's Collegiate Dictionary offers the following definitions:

White is - 1. The color of pure snow, light or comparatively light in color. 2. for, limited to, or predominantly made up of persons whose racial heritage is Caucasian: a White neighborhood.

3. politically conservative or reactionary. 4. auspicious; fortunate. 5. morally pure; innocent. 6. Lacking malice; harmless. 7. quality or state of being white. 8. opposite of black.

Black is – 1. Lacking hue and brightness. 2. Characterized by the absence of light. 3. a. pertaining or belonging to any of the dark-skinned peoples of Africa. b. African-American. 4. Soiled or stained with dirt. 5. Gloomy; pessimistic; dismal: a black future. 6. sullen or hostile. 7. Harmful; evil or wicked: a black heart.

Daniel Webster probably never meant for these definitions to be used in the context of how people think of each other. In all fairness, Webster and its staff define words according to how our society uses them. We all know America classifies people by the color of their skin, and the two dominant skin colors are Black and White. The Muslim minister in the movie Malcolm X vividly pointed out how America perceives the Black and White Races.

From another perspective, this scene vividly portrays the power of media.     One message the media sends is that White is clearly superior. White is beautiful and perfect and flawless, whether we are talking about soap or the hair color of a White woman. I wonder if Blacks were the majority in America, would the opposite be true? Remember, the majority doesn't control what the media projects; those in power over the media do.


### Can The Media Now Be Used To Educate Black Americans?

Yes! Every time I see Denzel Washington as a lawyer in the movie Philadelphia, as a news reporter in Pelican Brief, or as an XO (navy administrative officer) in Crimson Tide, I am proud to be a Black American. When I see Colin Powell addressing the Republican Party, I am overwhelmed with how far we have come in America.

The media continues to educate America, presenting us with the role models for this country. Black America badly needs to see itself in a positive light, to continue to improve its self-esteem and the way it thinks about itself. It needs to have as many positive Black role models as the media is willing to offer. Avery Brooks, the Captain in "Deep Space 9," one of the Star Trek television series, is a very positive role model. I am a true fan of this show. I feel that I am a part of something good when I see him making decisions that will protect and help other members of the space station. America is not yet at the point of this space station. One sign of when we've arrived will be when there is a television show about a successful Black businessperson…even if the show is a soap opera.

# Chapter
# 11

## Chapter Eleven - How Do You Communicate With Black Americans?

$\mathcal{B}$lacks in America have struggled to become educated in the way America thinks. Some of the way America thinks was in to the culture long before you or I were mere smiles on our mothers' faces. The fact is that Black Americans have worked for a long time to be included in the conversation that America has with her constituents.

American history is an important factor in being excluded. Because Black people had not been allowed to develop as a part of America's cultural exchange, we have a cultural deficit to overcome. Specifically, that deficit is our inability to communicate with the power structure or "system" that has been set up by the dominant culture. This may sound to you like I'm trying to excuse Black people for not fully assimilating into America. Not at all! I'm clarifying what White Americans need to know in order to communicate with Black Americans on an equitable basis.

Sidebar - Digression: A key word to understand is "equitable." Too often we talk about equality in America, but the total equality in a Capitalistic Society is an oxymoron. Equality to Americans is based on our rights, such as Civil Rights or the right to bear arms. All Americans in good standing with society can carry a gun, or be licensed to use a gun, as long as that use doesn't wrongfully harm a fellow American. But is this an equal right? Around 1997 a well-known Black American basketball player drove his expensive car, a "Hummer," with some Black friends to a paint ball tournament. Paintball guns look just like real guns.

They waved these guns around in the car as they drove down one of the most highly patrolled streets in the city Portland. (Yes, this was not a smart move.) They did not attempt to shoot the guns, nor did they aim the guns at anyone. The police were alerted to the situation, and pulled the Hummer over to the side of the road. Five patrol cars closed off the street. The would-be paintball players were arrested and cited for carrying the guns without a license. However, paintball guns do not require a license. The police defended their position by stating this was routine procedure for this type of the situation. Is this equality? Would White guys have received the same treatment? Maybe! But, Black American men driving around a public area with any type of a gun are practically guaranteed to be pulled over by the police and investigated, based on some type of standard procedure. Should these Black guys have known they were going to attract police attention? Yes, they should have known. Was this American equality at work? I am sure I can get a good argument going about whether these guys were treated in a manner equal to White counterparts. By the way, a local radio station dedicated two hours to a public debate over this instance.

Equity exists if we all have the same *opportunity* to have an experience, gain knowledge, etc. We Americans like to associate opportunity with success, but it also means opportunity to fail. Some people might argue that the example with the would-be paintball players and the police depicted equitable treatment. The guys in the Hummer were treated the same way any group of White guys would have been under the same set of circumstances. In summary, I define equity as the ability for someone to have an opportunity to fully participate in the glorious success of America no matter how they look, think, believe or speak. (End digression.)

The preceding digression sets the stage for an explanation of how White Americans and Black Americans can better communicate with each other. The secret ingredient to communication between White and Black America is equitable education. It is paramount with regard to how people interact and how to improve relationships.

The very first thing that White America needs to understand about Black America is we have not had equitable educational opportunities. We are still the first generation of Black Americans just getting in and through the education system. As I explained in the chapters on thinking and assimilation, anyone who did not get educated in America has a serious deficit for communicating with Americans. The ability to process information in the American way is paramount to living and being successful in America. Communicating in America is the most important thing to learn. This has been the biggest challenge for Black America—our ability to think and communicate with White America. The burden to understand and communicate with White America has been on Black America. This has been and will continue to be true for a long time. Black Americans continue to make great strides to fix or close this communication gap, but there is a lot of work yet to be done. Too often we have had to demand this communication, and therein lie the problem.

### What Must White America Do To Communicate With Black America?

First, accept Black thinking as a part of the American thinking process. You and I know that in America we think in a European way, that is, we connect certain ideas together, classify concepts in certain ways, and follow particular trains of thought. Very much egalitarian! Anyone in America who doesn't think in a European way had better learn. This is quite arrogant on the part of White Americans, that if a person doesn't process in a Eurocentric line of thinking, that person is stupid or ignorant. I am not saying that this is a bad line of thinking. It is just one-sided and exclusionary. It hinders communication.

Second, White Americans need learn to understand Black American thinking. I have tried my best to present this book from a White American perspective. But I have worked to avoid having it come from a Eurocentric thinking perspective. Although I have used editors who are White Americans and native English speakers, they are outside their own basic ways of thinking when communicating with Black Americans. I realize that trying to get outside of our own basic thinking can be incredibly difficult. I have trouble when I have to deal with Asians or Hispanics, even my wife, because she is female. I work very hard to compensate for my shortcomings and my inability to communicate with the rest of the world that is different from me. I struggle with my own American arrogance, and the feeling of being superior because I am American. Add my Christian beliefs to that and you have a real religious, egotistical, maniac on your hands. (Laugh!) Communications can be very one-sided if a person's thinking process is narrowly American. The pilgrims were much like me when they arrive on Plymouth Rock. They believed they could make life better for themselves and the rest of the world. To be a focused thinker often leads one to narrow thinking. And anyone who has been successful doing – or thinking – things in a certain way will be harder to change. But, I purport that our thinking is flawed if it excludes a people.

### What Language Do Black Americans Speak?

To say that there is only one way to communicate in America is to delude ourselves. Language is more than a tool to verbalize what we are thinking; it is also a part of a set of tools to fully communicate with other humans. Classroom English is not the only way to speak English. White America has deemed it the correct way to communicate. I must admit, I have been indoctrinated into speaking English as White as I can. Keep in mind I graduated from a University that was predominantly White in the northwestern part of the United States. In spite of their efforts to simply educate us, universities teach and indoctrinate us as to what – and how – we should think.

If one group forces everyone to communicate only in one way, then all groups are not really communicating with each other. White America owns the way America has communicated for the last 300 years. Black Americans have been kept from learning and participating in that communication until the last 50 years. The good news is, there has been tremendous progress, but not as rapidly as we would like them to be.

Black Americans speak English, but in two dialects. They really do not have much choice in the matter. Many Blacks learned to speak English out of necessity and through access to education systems that were setup and defined by White Americans. They learned to use English as a tool to communicate, and not as the thinking process, as it so often is today. Languages and accents are powerful cultural stabilizers and are very hard to change, even with the power of education. Compared to other cultures in America, Black Americans have much greater challenges in trying to assimilate. This is because they have a hard time believing that a process that for so long excluded them is now working for them.

Black Americans are uneasy speaking in the proper English of the northwest. When I go to New Orleans or other southern cities and speak proper English, everyone points out that I am *trying* to talk "proper". The comment may also suggest some envy mixed with a subtle compliment that I had risen to the level of proficiency and status that goes with being successful in America. They are not telling me that this is wrong in the Black community. Instead, they are saying, do not come into this community thinking you are more than those of us who have remained here. These people either haven't had opportunities or, if they have, have chosen to maintain a language that blends with the New Orleans Black community culture.

In time we will learn to speak in the manner required by America. Blacks do understand the value of speaking English in the manner of newscasters, they just don't believe that it is a necessity. In the American school systems, one of the first things teachers attempt to do is to teach students how to write with correct grammar. Most Black students jump in with two feet. However, they don't give up the Black American dialects easily.

### Can White Americans Have Non-Confrontational Conversations With Black America?

Black and White Americans do have normal conversations all the time. But, Whites who have not had a lot of experience interacting with Blacks are often very uncomfortable during the initial verbal conversations. I believe this is because White America is uncomfortable dealing with Black America and that results in a stiff, distant air to settle onto Black and White communications.

For communication to improve between Black and White America there have to be many more positive interactions. Like everything else in the world, both groups need opportunities to practice and build skills. These skills should enable us to erase some of the impediments that make us not trust each other. The ability to communicate across cultures is an important and highly sought-after skill in America. By this time in our history, it should be standard operating procedure. Instead, it is often quid pro quo, a few interactions that are positive and the rest are merely perfunctory.

It is so neat to see large crowds of Americans get excited about Michael Jordan, Steve Young, or Kristi Yamaguchi, or Whitney Houston. Americans truly like our stars. This enthusiasm for people of diverse backgrounds diminishes when we deal with each other on a day-to-day basis. An extreme example is Madison, Chicago whose residents refuse to accept Black Americans moving into the community. Oddly enough, any Blacks who could afford to move to Madison were successful professionals. These Madison White Americans stopped going to the mall out of fear that they might get mugged. In contrast to their fears, investigative reporting revealed that life had not changed and, in fact, had improved for the local residents during the time that Blacks had moved in. In spite of this, the negative perceptions of the White residents were so high that they would not allow themselves to be convinced, and they were blind to how their neighborhoods had grown culturally rich due to the influx of Blacks in the community.

To build up a bank of trust, White Americans must give Black Americans every opportunity possible to participate in wholesome, trusting communication. This is not easy. Many Black Americans will reject these overtures, as they will be skeptical of your efforts. They had to learn to be cautious, based on centuries of interaction with White America. As you read in chapter 6, in the past and still today, Black Americans have had many negative experiences with White Americans. Currently, White Americans continue to exhibit a silent lack of acceptance to have Black Americans in their neighborhoods and in their daily lives. Although the rationale for this is evident, nobody likes it. Americans want our lives to be "la-de-da," but we don't want to leave our comfort zones to help people who are not like us. Human nature? Maybe! American nature? For sure!

### *Is There Room For Informational Exchange Between Black And White Americans?*

If America is to be successful within its own borders, she will have to freely share information between Black and White Americans. This would be good! America will always be challenged by how well it communicates within its systems and structures. It shouldn't assume that everyone, those born here as well as those who immigrated to this land, can understand what is happening within our borders, no matter how simple it may seem.

This country has grown into a complex monolithic social and economic system. These systems only continue to work if they are self-sustaining. The United States has learned to sustain itself by making sure that it has social services that sustain its citizens, regardless of their educational status. Not only are we a country of people that innovate and are technically savvy, but we now also depend on technology for almost everything we do. This recent dependence on technology is just one more reason we need to pay attention to each other.

Once, Black Americans were dependent on White Americans. But this is no longer true. Blacks have learned to use – and depend on – technology as much as White Americans do. However, White America continues to control and manage most of the systems that drive the economics of our nation. In the meanwhile, Black Americans continue to learn the steps of Assimilation pointed out in chapter 4, especially steps 3 – to gain a source of income, 5 – become educated in the American thinking process, and 6 – owning a piece of the land. These steps will pull Black America deeper into the American culture. One of the results is that more Blacks will become technically savvy. America's technological dependence means that it will rely more and more on the technically savvy citizen – Black or White – to maintain, improve, and adapt our systems. In summary, our increasing need for technology will also help propel the Black assimilation process.

As the country that sets the standard for lifestyle and quality of living, America will continue to see other countries emulate us and challenge us. Many peoples and nations depend on us to move the world forward. To be a role model as a country, we should demonstrate open and vital communications at and between every socioeconomic group. The world looks to us, and America is the experiment that they hope will be even more successful. Black and White America have made great progress in communicating and educating the world in terms of bringing together two large races. I am confident that we can make this work for us, and provide the model for the rest of the world!

# Chapter
# 12

## Chapter Twelve - Can We Americans Solve The Biggest Problem In Our Country: Racism?

*I* was walking through the Salt Lake City Airport when I spotted a T-shirt with this saying:

*"None of us is as good as all of us!"*

I have never encountered a saying that was so short yet so complete. It sums up all I want to say in this chapter. For America to continue to be a great place to live and work, it will have to build a trusting relationship between White and Black Americans. I believe it will continue to focus on this task, but it will often have to be prompted and encouraged. And the only way we can ever fully realize a trusting relation between the Blacks and Whites in America is to continue to solve the problem of racism.

What Is Racism? Can you touch it? Smell it? Taste It? Hear It? See it? Think about It? Experience It? Explain it? Define it?

It is very important not to confuse racism with racist behavior. Racism is much more damaging than racist behavior, with which it is often confused. All of us have displayed racist behavior at some point in our lives. But all of us do not display the results of Racism. Racism is not burning a church or calling someone a negative racial name. Burning a church or calling someone a negative name can be behaviors that are the result of racism. Many Black Americans are racist, but they rarely practice racism. If you understand these fundamental concepts, you are well on your way to understanding one of the most powerful forces at work in America. The effects of racism in America are destructive to this wonderful nation. Frequently, Black and White Americans don't understand the true definition of racism. When a young white kid first thinks that he is smarter or better than his Black peer, racism is beginning to manifest itself. In this case, only one is aware that something is awry. When a White kid decides to put this thinking into practice, perhaps to try to gain an advantage over a Black kid, he is practicing racism.

Racism is a problem we have lived with since America was born. In the first chapter, Black and White Americans got off to a real bad start, historically speaking. And from there, we went down hill for 200 years. I believe we are now going up hill, and most of our progress has occurred during the last 50 years. Every time I see my daughter with her high school friends and the members of her volley ball, track and/or soccer team, I know we are making progress. (Most of my children's friends are White.) My son is as open-minded to all people as can be. They both encourage me, and reaffirm my hope for America. Despite the progress over the last fifty years, there is still much work to be done. The good news is that this work will get done, because we all know that Americans have the will, time, and resources to do it.

## Definition Of Racism

According to the Webster dictionary, racism is a belief that race is the primary determinant of human traits and capacities and that racial differences produce an inherent superiority of a particular race.

## I define racism as follows:

**Racism a condition of human nature that is brought about by a dominant race, often in the majority, gaining social and economic POWER, which allows them to oppress another race, resulting in significant to total domination of the oppressed race's culture.**

When I presented these two definitions of racism to a class of international graduate level business students, their discussion consisted of acknowledging how differently we have seen and experienced life with regard to race. Amazingly, most people don't agree on the definition of racism. Most people define it in terms of their past experiences, regardless of whether or not they are a part of the race that is the oppressor or the oppressed. Although most of us agree that racism is a terrible thing, at any given time, we can't agree on how terrible a situation is.

Many Americans are unsure as to whether or not they participate in racism, and are often in denial as to whether they are part of the oppressors or the oppressed. Forgive me, but here is my conclusion:

**Are We All Participants In Racism?**

This is true, because racism has become such an integral part of the American life and thought process, as discussed earlier. After you finish reading this sentence, stop, and assess your own thinking. Define racism as it pertains to you.

STOP And THINK!.................

Did you scare yourself? If you didn't, you lied to yourself, and you should repeat the exercise trying to be as honest with yourself as you possibly can. I scare myself all the time in terms of how much I participate in implementing racism, knowing it is not only going to adversely affect someone else, but also adversely affect me. The scary thing about racism is, I practice it because of my success in America.

As an executive assistant to a city commissioner (a White American woman), I was responsible for managing her staff, including hiring and firing. For some of my first assignments, the commissioner asked me to fire several of her staff members. I agreed to do so. One staff member was a White American woman. After a number of years working together, she and the commissioner had reached a point where they simply got on each other's nerves. I treated this woman in such a way as to send the message that she was no longer in the good graces of the commissioner. In our dialogues, I would include questions about whether or not this was the right place for her to be working. She got the hint and, finally, quit.

I then started to build a case to fire another staff member who was a Black American woman, but in this case I concluded that we were doing the right thing for the wrong reasons. This individual was capable of doing the job, but was very frustrated, because she believed that she should have been promoted on the basis of the length of time that she had been on this job. She had begun to complain a lot, so that her attitude was poor, while the quality of her work remained relatively good. I thought about what I had learned about stereotypes of Black people, and realized that the commissioner had fallen into the trap of thinking of this worker in this way. We did not have good grounds to fire her based on performance. Instead, we were concluding she was lazy--just another Black woman who didn't have a good work ethic. Eventually, I did document a solid case to fire her. However, this time the commissioner got cold feet and we didn't fire her. The irony of this story is, I was fired by the commissioner a couple of months later for the right reasons: I did not like my job. Before I left, I reflected on the situation and asked the commissioner if she might be a racist. She admitted she might be.

Racism is often based on different attitudes, mostly stereotypic thinking. In today's America, this can be constructed on difference and history. We will discuss how we American got to these poor attitudes, shortly.

## *Has Racism Been With Us in America From The Beginning?(Historical Racism)*

In his book White Over Black: American Attitudes toward the Negro, 1550-1812, Winthrop D. Jordan discusses how the Englishman of early America responded negatively to Africans, even during the initial, casual contact as part of an exploration. The English believed African blackness was strange, troublesome, and even repugnant. Talk about getting off to a bad start. When the lightest-skinned people of the world came face to face with the darkest-skinned people of the world, this difference resulted in a very negative impression. Jordan adds that blackness was already a symbol to convey some of the most ingrained values of English society. Black and its opposite White were emotion-laden words. Black meant foul, dirty, wicked, malignant, and disgraceful. It signified night, which was a time of fear and uncertainty. The English language is full of these definitions and expressions, such as having a black mark on your record. Black is associated with darkness, a place where evil lurks. Another expression is a person can be blackballed in the financial world. White on the other hand is chastity, virtue, beauty, and peace. Women are married in white to symbolize purity and virginity. White is holy and angelic. Is this starting to make sense? Racism was the result of fear, which had developed because of a clash of differences. Fear, as we discussed earlier, is a powerful emotion that can bring about many bad results. (Much of this discussion was taken from the book, The Great Fear, edited by Gary B. Nash/Richard Weiss, 1970.)

# Chapter 12

## *What Is The Psychology Of Racism In America?*

***Social, economic, political, and religious factors have influenced numerous interactions over the last 400 years, building into racial ideologies for White and Black Americans. Throughout this time period, racism has become embedded in our institutions at all levels.***

As author Peter Loewenberg points out in <u>The Great Fear</u>, racism is both extremely personal and social in origin. It is marbled into the deepest parts of our social consciousness. It influences a multitude of the decisions made in America. It manifests itself through these attitudes to result in devastating actions.

How did we get these attitudes? All behavior is learned behavior. Without learned behavior, there is no action. One type of behavior is prejudice. Prejudice is the seed that racism grows from. Just as we eat and drink, we learn to pre-judge things. Some of us love to eat eggs, and others are sickened by the very thought of eggs. When behavior is fueled by how we feel about something, a system of thinking develops. All systems of thinking eventually corroborate reality, or the perception of reality. At times, the perception of reality may contradict reality. For example, if the economy is bad, we don't ask ourselves why the revenues for an organization or industry sector have been low. Instead, we consider the mitigating circumstances and conclude that the economy is bad, because the government has not controlled the deficit and interest rates. We use the same mechanism to bring about prejudice. The crime rate in the neighborhood is going up, it must be because Blacks moved into the neighborhood.

Today, White Americans can blame their forefathers for creating and developing the system of thinking that Black Americans are inferior to White Americans. This system of thinking is reinforced by self-perpetuating experiences. That is, the media reports the crime statistics and they continue to show that Blacks are proportionally committing more crimes than other racial groups. Chapter two contained statistics that validate some of this type of media reporting. A thousand years ago, powerful Black kings ruled Egypt; 300 years ago, Blacks were slaves in America; today, Blacks are quickly approaching complete assimilation into America. The road to this progress is bumpy, but we are making significant progress.

When systems of thinking and behaviors continuously influence each other, Lowenberg says the result is a "self-fulfilling prophecy." If I learned to think of someone as inferior to me when I was a child and then learned how to exert influence over that person's actions, I will continue to perceive that person as inferior, reinforcing my original premise. If I classify that person with everyone who looks and acts like him or her, I have formed a stereotype about that group of people. From this stereotype, I may develop an attitude, then act in accordance with that attitude, resulting in prejudice and RACISM. Racism needs a power source to survive and grow so that it transfers itself from thinking to action. In America, Whites have an economic power source that is inexhaustible – if Whites choose not to share economic power, the result can be years of racial oppression. Circumstances such as riots, revolutions, and wars may alleviate the oppression, but absolute power will prevail.

Black and White children play a key role in reinforcing these negative racial attitudes in America. These children internalize the values that are modeled in front of them. If the dominant group establishes systems and mores that keep another group in an inferior position in terms of their ability to learn and experience life, the superior/inferior attitudes become ingrained in both those groups' attitudes. I scare myself to think that if I had remained in my old neighborhood and had lost hope that I might have participated in burning the neighborhood. I love and care about many White Americans, but I honestly love other Black Americans and myself more. To help you understand this sentiment, we Americans would fight to protect American shores if we believed we were threatened as a people.

Inequities remain in our present day society: Black Americans still struggle to be accepted as gifted business people, managers, or community leaders. The more educated we Black Americans become, the more we recognize these inequities. We have learned to wield our knowledge into power that we try to apply to change this imbalance. However, using this power and knowledge may not result in productive dialogue and progress. Instead, using power to try to effect change without concurrence by all groups involved can result in destruction. This is evident throughout our history in wars, including racial wars, as people realize that their differences cannot be resolved by reason. If knowledge results in hate, we all lose. This is the only aspect of America that scares me. We must find ways to bring about fair and equitable use of America's resources and, hence, its wealth and success.

### *Is Racism Still As Powerful A Force Today As It Was Before? (Modern Day Racism)*

A person who knows that he or she is prevented from accomplishing a goal solely because of being a part of the minority will become very frustrated. Black people in America are frustrated, because they are not accepted into all levels of our society and economies.

In some ways racism is more powerful today than it was in yesteryears. As mentioned above, Black Americans are becoming more educated and consequently more aware of the inequities of society. They have started to analyze the "whats and the whys." What and why something is not available to us. Tiger Woods can play golf anywhere in the world. Economically, he couldn't afford to play in many tournaments without turning professional. I can't play at many golf courses because the club charters don't allow Blacks, not the written charters, but the charters that reflect their attitudes. Even if a club's policy was relaxed to include Blacks, we Blacks believe that club members wouldn't really want us there. Tiger is personally changing this in the best way possible, by commanding the American media to pay attention and by convincing White American businessmen that Black is good business. He has revolutionized the game of golf so that it will never again be thought of as a game only rich White Americans can play. Finally, Tiger has helped Blacks change their own thinking, no longer is golf a boring, stupid game played by retired old White men.

Racism is as prevalent as ever in America today. Evidence lies in the mixed messages from our government with regard to who can play in politics and business, specifically the challenges to affirmative action. The government used to try to neutralize the inequities of society. The Supreme Court has diluted Affirmative Action; the result is that the government is sending mixed and confusing messages to Blacks. The messages encourage level playing fields, but no longer discourage inequities. Black Americans are finally starting to understand the assimilation process and are trying to build their own sources of income and resources. Just as we started to come into our own, the laws that helped us overcome discrimination were changed. Teaching people to make bread but not allowing them to practice long enough to perfect their skill sounds like another broken promise to Black Americans.

The workplace exhibits more racism than ever. Many corporations continue to discriminate against Blacks on the grounds that they do not have enough education or experience. Once, a college degree was required to enter a technical field, now the requirement is a master's degree. What came first, the chicken or the egg? Blacks were blocked from the workplace for the last 50 years, and we are now in the doorway. We no longer need descriptive hiring. We can now succeed on our own. But, they can't get promoted, because we don't have enough experience to qualify for management. I continue to look at my desk at a stack of articles about various companies who have been caught discriminating against Blacks. Jessie Jackson continues to go to the boardrooms of corporate America pleading the case. I wish he wouldn't just settle for money and do more to convince corporate CEO's that they need Black Americans in their workforce.

Sidebar - Digression: I read an article that described a new form of racism. Some White Americans who are in power were convincing non-Black ethnic minorities that Blacks are hurting the other minorities' efforts to obtain equity. The article ("Politics is no longer merely a matter of Black and White," The Oregonian, Sunday, December 15, 1996) described a White woman who unseated a Black woman on Oakland's City Council by taking advantage of redistricting designed to give Hispanic and Asian Americans more voice. During her campaign the White woman convinced her Asian and Hispanic constituents that she was better for them than the Black incumbent was. Remember that redistricting should have resulted in a Hispanic or Asian City Council candidate. End sidebar

Racism has always been prevalent throughout American society. It used to be laden with hate and discontent; now it is made of frustration and confusion. The results of this racism can be more devastating in the end. It will result in a people coming to the conclusion that the system can no longer be changed, and they will lose hope. This racism will have dire consequences for all American people.

### Has Racism Become A Part of The Practical Side Of Our Country? (Practical Racism)

Racism is often very practical. Let me discuss an institution that is very near and dear to me. That institution is the church. When do many Americans join large groups of people who are similar to each other? Sunday Morning! The most segregated time in America is Sunday Morning. On Sunday we retreat to commune with and worship our Maker. Many consider this the most precious and uplifting time of our week. Frequently, we choose to do this with people who look, think, and sing just as we do. The singing part is very important, because it represents a cultural difference between the White and Black race. Although time spent in church is generally considered sacred and joyous, it actually is practical racism. There is no thought of anything racial, including racial enmity. We simply forget that other races and ethnicities exist. The irony is that the precious time we spend in church is actually sanctioned for segregation.

When I was in the IBM Corporation, we were trained to manage everything, including the way people joined the company. We tested everyone that joined the firm during the 80's. If I recall, the test was a psychological test that tested the thinking ability of the perspective candidate. But this test discriminated against many people of color. The courts examined this test and determined that it did not result in enough discrimination to preclude IBM from using it. Last I heard, IBM was still using this test. Racism was practical for IBM, and so IBM continues to practice it.

### *What Effects Does Racism Have On Our American Economy? (The Economics Of Racism)*

Racism is a very powerful mechanism in America. It is most damaging when it is allowed to flourish in the economic, social, and educational systems in America. When people are not given the opportunity to self-actualize (self-actualize means being as resourceful as possible or permitted) those people will not be able to contribute to their potential, and America will be cheated of potential resources.

Racism short-circuits the economy. Our financial systems require resources be used to their full capacity. The government has programs that assist Black Americans in starting businesses. But the government doesn't have any good programs to assist these minority start-ups in exerting an influence within their business sectors. Black businesses that are in technical fields often have difficulty finding Black resources to fuel further growth. What started as a Black dollar ends up a White dollar! Black-owned businesses often have a large proportion of White Americans on staff. This is not bad in and of itself, but it drains resources from Black communities.

As long as the Black community cannot sustain itself, it will continue to be a drain on America's economy. We Americans must understand that our business activities depend on all of us being successful. One of us is not successful unless all of us are successful, or progressing toward success. The economy can only afford to be good to all us, whether we succeed or fail equitably. Please don't think of this as a socialistic approach. I am a capitalist down to my bone marrow. But, I am also a realistic observer of systems and, as long as a system fails one of us, it will continue to fail all us in some manner. How long will it take to overcome 300 years of racial prejudice?

Although I cannot answer this question, I hope we can someday truly overcome racism. We are making great strides in some areas. Racism does not exist when we examine our thoughts and actions and thoughts to test them for any adverse affect on others who are not of our ethnicity, culture, or our race. White Americans carry most of the power for racism and that gives you the most effective weapon against racism. In other words the very thing that fuels racism is the same thing that shuts it down — power.

# Chapter
# 13

## Chapter Thirteen – Do Americans Want Racial Reconciliation?

$\mathcal{R}$acial relations between Black and White America have greatly improved. The state of racism in America was examined in the previous chapter. I believe we all agree that Racism is alive and well, growing in some areas and improving in others. Many movements attempt to improve relations between White and Black America. The President of the United States has made it a top agenda item for the government. Specifically, President Clinton has convened a seven-member committee of some of the nation's top experts and academicians to provide recommendations as to how to continue to reconcile the races. As expected, this committee is struggling to decide on a focus and process, namely, how to be fair to all the committee members. However, the committee's charter is to be fair, to represent all the different views on the committee, and to start a dialogue on Race Relations in America. I predict that the committee will not reach unanimous consensus, because each member is trying to represent every American. I believe they will eventually realize they need to break this approach down into the basic causes of our problems. I just hope they don't continue to spend all their time on problem definition.

Previously, I introduced you to a group called the Promise Keepers. Racial reconciliation is so important to the members of this group that they have made it one of the seven promises they commit to keep before God. As a Christian I join the millions of other American Christian men in believing that this is a promise that is worth keeping. I applaud their efforts. They are making great strides at a root level in reconciliation, specifically, to reach out and include each other, even before dialogue begins. I hope they don't forget the dialogue.

At this point, I will define reconciliation.

**Reconciliation (Unger)** - the restoration to friendship and fellowship after estrangement. This definition of reconciliation contains the idea of atonement for past sin. To change from one position to a totally different one. (This definition does not identify who was bad, good, wrong, or right.) Reconciliation, therefore, means that someone or something is completely altered in order to meet a required standard. (Unger, 1980 Moody Press)

Unger is a biblical dictionary. The Black American – as well as the White American – value system primarily comes from a Christian perspective.

**Reconciliation (Webster)** – **1.** The act of reconciling or the state of being reconciled. 2. The process of making consistent or compatible.

*To completely understand this, Webster's definition of reconcile follows below.*

**Reconcile (Webster)** – to cause (a person) to accept or be resigned to something not desired. 2. To cause to become friendly or peaceable again: to reconcile hostile persons 3. To compose or settle (a quarrel, dispute, etc.). 4. To bring into agreement or harmony; make compatible or consistent: to reconcile accounts. 5. To restore. 6. To be reconciled.

Based on these definitions, for racial reconciliation in Americans we must first admit that Black and White Americans are not friends and are out of fellowship. We don't trust each other. We don't want to live near each other. We don't care to socialize with each other, and we don't like, or even hate, each other. If this were 1953, the year I was born, all of the above would be true for most

Americans. But this is the late 1990's, and we are in a world that is learning it needs to live in harmony to have a high quality of life. I surmise that many of us believe that we are in the process of reconciling. But for many others, the conditions of 1953 still exist, causing impatience, frustration, and an impetus for change. Perhaps we need to start by admitting that "we don't understand each other." Admitting we don't understand is indeed our next step.

Promise Keepers have skipped this step. They have gone to a mediator, which, in this case, is religious belief. Specifically, they agree that God would not have claim to love our brother while we actually hate him. To resolve this, they have opted to use a strategy of inclusion, and it appears to be working. They are able to find common ground in worshiping their loving God, whom they believe requires them to love all of their brothers and sisters. But this does not mean that the reconciliation process is traveling smoothly down the yellow brick road. Every one of these brothers return to mostly segregated churches on Sunday morning and sings songs like "I Love You Lord." They keep the promise at the rally and during other Promise Keepers activities. Promise Keepers now has the big job of trying to acculturate the church, which I believe, is ready to be acculturated. All of this is heading in the right direction and I like what I see so far.

There are numerous other organizations that encourage us to improve race relations in America. Part of the YWCA mission is to include all races and ethnic groups. Although the YWCA holds annual forums on diversity, like everyone else, it tackles too many problems at once. I applaud the Y's efforts and hope it continues to pursue inclusion.

Racial reconciliation has not yet been discussed in thousands of other organizations and systems that promote good will among people. How does this all manifest itself in this day and age? As denial that there is a problem. Many Americans are solidly in this stage of denial.

# Chapter 13

## *Do Black Americans Want Racial Reconciliation?*

Yes, more than anything in the world, but they have no real concrete methods to bring about racial healing in our nation. We Blacks know we are a part of the problem, but will quickly point out we did not cause it. With that attitude, progress in this area will be harder to make. We Black Americans may be a bigger problem than we are willing to admit. We are still trying to convince you White Americans that we are Americans, just as you are, and we spend a tremendous amount of time trying to convince you that we are your equal! We often send you messages that are hard to understand, and all you can do is give us that enigmatic smile you use when lost for words. We do not need to be equal in America; we need to have equity in America. Equity means obtaining education and having access to the American dream.

Black Americans are convinced that we can do everything you can do as well or better, and without help from White Americans. Over time, Black Americans learned that they will fail if they rely on White America. While this has often been true, it is less so in the present. This line of thought will drive all of us to the edge of an impasse, trying to reconcile racial differences when we refuse to work together. Black Americans try to ignore White Americans in every way possible, but White Americans are our partners, and we need each other. Much of the American social contract has been influenced by the relationships between Black and White America.

Reconciling the White and Black Americans is the goal, not the process. Black Americans must be assured they are not trying alone. White Americans must be encouraged to try for their own sake, rather than as an attempt to atone for the past. White America does not need to be convinced to accept Black America; they already do. Instead, both races need to realize we are stuck with each other and must learn to live together. We know we are all Americans and it is time to rally the troops to create peace, not war.

Black Americans expect to a write a new page in history describing Black American accomplishments and how they have helped all Americans. The page would describe new Black media role models such as:

- Avery Brooks playing the role of the Captain of the Defiant on "Star Trek: Deep Space Nine."
- Denzel Washington featured as an Administrative Officer of a nuclear powered submarine.
- Vanessa Williams co-starring in a movie with Arnold Schwartzenegger.
- James Earl Jones playing the role of Admiral Greer in three top-grossing films of the nineties based on novels written by Tom Clancy.

This represents progress, although even in the area of Hollywood movies, Black Americans still have a way to go. We can be very proud when we see Colin Powell speak at the Republican convention, knowing he understands what it means to be a Black American. Although many Americans wanted Colin Powell to run for President in the 1996 elections, he declined, stating he was not ready to be president. I was afraid if he ran, someone would try to kill him. I also believe that America was not ready to have Colin Powell, or any other Black American, as President.

Although Black Americans are ready to reconcile with White Americans, they are scared of what reconciliation may cost. Throughout our history, many Blacks have died to bring about social and economic change. As a result, Whites may have to drag them, kicking and screaming, into reconciliation until they realize nobody is trying to harm them.

## *Do White Americans Want Racial Reconciliation?*

Most White Americans would look quizzically if you asked this question, followed by a long pause, throat-clearing noises. Finally, they would launch into something like the following dissertation.

"We have always wanted Black Americans to live in peace and harmony and to have nothing but best in America. We just want them to earn it the way we did. We want them to understand that there are no free rides, and the only way you get anything in America is by 'blood, sweat and tears,' which equates to hard work. The results must have all three ingredients if you are to be successful. Black Americans spend too much time worrying about what White Americans think, say, and do. They have need to get going with their own lives, and move this process forward for themselves!"

Do you, as a White American, agree with that this little dissertation is fairly accurate in capturing the mood of White America?

Many White Americans have led the fight for equal rights, knowing that, at best, they could only achieve some semblance of acceptance and minimal civil rights. These Whites believed they were working toward reconciliation, but they were really trying to right the wrongs of their ancestors. Regardless, they did, and continue to, accomplish a lot. In the end, much of this work did count to move all of us a little closer toward reconciliation.

White Americans are just starting to understand the plight of Black America, even over the last twenty years. As a consequence, White Americans are now comfortable questioning the status quo. For instance, Whites were able to discuss their discomfort when more than two Black families move within a square mile of their subdivision. As previously noted, in Madison, Illinois, Whites started to move out of a posh neighborhood, because too many Black families moved in. When interviewed on national television, these Whites shared how they stopped shopping at the local mall, because they were afraid of being mugged by upper-middle class Black youth. Interestingly, they admitted they knew nobody had been mugged at the mall since the Black families moved in. Regardless, they were still afraid. This attitude is difficult for Black Americans to understand.

Similarly, the White American church would probably say that they want reconciliation between White and Black America. I believe the White church congregations of America really believe they want racial reconciliation. I do not believe they have asked themselves what the cost of reconciliation would be. They haven't yet significantly tested a strategy to accomplish this. Church congregations reflect a type of segregation, since they are generally comprised of people with similar socio-economic and racial backgrounds. It will take many humble hearts to comprehend what full reconciliation will mean. The main mission of the Apostle Paul was to convince people to live for Christ. He also worked hard to destroy the wall of enmity between Jew and Gentile and that they could live, work, play and worship together. However, within the greater Christian church, the primary separation has been along doctrinal lines. Stated in the converse, sharing common beliefs has been a major factor in bringing together people of different racial and ethnic backgrounds.

Along with many Black Americans, many White Americans will have to be dragged, kicking and screaming, to the reconciliation table. But, you will do it. You will make it happen, and you will work hard at it. Yes, harder than Black Americans, due to the fact you have more to gain in the end. You know that you have the power and that power can be used to make all of our lives better in America.

### *Do Other Ethnic Races Want Racial Reconciliation Between White And Black America?*

It is my belief that non-Black ethnic minorities would also love to have racial reconciliation between White and Black Americans. They know it would benefit them to fix the worst part of the racial problem. After this, reconciling with other racial and ethnic groups should be much easier. I believe the racial rifts between other ethnic minorities and White Americans are not as wide as the one between White and Black Americans. Previously, we explored many reasons why the rift is wider between Black and White Americans. The first and foremost reason is Blacks have lived longer in America, and their problems have therefore more deeply imprinted into our history. (The Native American has been here equally as long as Black and White Americans, but have now dwindle to numbers that make their plight lesser numerically.)

Many other ethnic minorities disagree that the plight of the Black American has been worse than any other groups. This dissention hinders reconciliation between the ethnic races of America. Recently, minorities have been vying to be the most powerful minority in America. This is a new twist to an old problem. This competition will be irrelevant, if White and Black America do not reconcile. Other ethnic minorities seek the same equities as most Black Americans do. They want also access to government and economic power. I am amazed at how non-White Americans scramble for the crumbs on the American floor, while we could stand up and take what we need from the table. Sadly, walls of enmity have grown between the various ethnic Americans.

A few years ago, I would have included the Italians, Swedes, Irish and the other European ethnic groups in this discussion. However, these groups have blended into the majority as to be fairly indistinguishable. At one time, they, too, faced ostracism, prejudice, and exclusion from access to governmental power and economic authority. Now, they have won these, but at a price. These distinguishing characteristics of these cultures have been reduced to observing holidays and festival celebrations on certain days of the years.

## *What Are The Components Of Solutions That Work?*

Black and White Americans need to develop a plan that will foster discussion about simple solutions. Promise Keepers has demonstrated how to start. They brought people together who share a common ground, in this case faith, with the purpose of accomplishing a goal, honoring promises.

Finding the common ground for racial reconciliation is vital to start the communication process. Different groups have different bases for common grounds. Promise Keepers participants share their Christian faith. Government programs appeal to people's needs to share resources. Youth organizations try to tie together people on the basis of a common age group. I like every one of these reasons, because they all get us out of the rut. There are plenty of reasons to work hard to reconcile White and Black America. The biggest reason is we live, work and play in the best country in the world.

A word of caution about common grounds is in order. Promise Keepers may run into a conflict of different perceptions of the racial problem based on different personal histories. This may occur in any of the groups mentioned above. I encourage you all to stay the course and weather the storm. Our goal is fixed, reconciliation, but the process will change and adapt, as we learn more. Continue to question the efficacy of what each group is doing, and be willing to change, if needed. And remind yourselves that you are doing this, because it is the right thing to do and the benefits are overwhelming.

**StepsTowards Lasting Reconciliation.**

**Step1.** White supremacy has to cease. This will be hard to stop. It is the fabric of racial indifference. An example of white supremacy is when caring White Americans think they are better than their fellow Black Americans. If a person thinks he or she is better, then he or she will act accordingly. This will smother acceptance on the spot.

**Step 2.** We must continue to dialogue about our differences in order to understand what is important to each other. This dialogue will enable an exchange of a large quantity of information, which, in turn, will help us to educate each other and understand each other.

**Step 3.** We must spend more quality time together in groups that are racially diverse but share common beliefs and values. Promise Keepers has been successful at the spiritual and emotional level. This step will help break down social barriers, which will help to break down economic barriers, such as restrictions to professional opportunities.

**Step 4.** We need to love and have compassion for each other. This will grow out of step 3, and help reduce interracial barriers.

**Step 5.** We are going to have to risk more with each other. Specifically, this means being willing to change the roles of the traditional leaders and followers in business. When the groups that once were followers start to also become business leaders, they start to obtain some of the wealth of the land. In the past, this has happened for the Italians, Germans, Jews, and Irish.

Reconciliation is the final part of the healing process for relationships on a personal level. We will need a lot of patience, if we are to be successful in our efforts to lead America to its true potential. Everyone must contribute. Each one of us must find a way to obtain the key ingredient, trust.

# Chapter
## 14

### Chapter Fourteen – Can Black American Youth Survive the Status Quo?

$\mathcal{A}$ merica's most important mission is to prepare our children for the future. But we have a critical failing in achieving this mission, losing a significant portion of Black youth. We are losing our Black youth from society faster than any other segment of the population. They are being lost to death and imprisonment. Homicide is the leading cause of death for young Black American males. As stated previously, many young Black American men have been incarcerated and near-term forecasts indicate as many as 32% more will be incarcerated, as compared to 7% of young White American men. (Data source: the Sentencing Project, 1996.) This is an alarming statistic. The New York Times describes Black American youth this way:

"They are the children of the shadows: the impoverished youth who live in tumble down neighborhoods of the American inner city; the children of often desperate and broken families, where meals are sometimes cereal three times a day; the young people who face the lure of drugs, sex, fast money and guns; the unnoticed youths who operate in a maddening universe where things always seem to go wrong...Numbers and trends tell only so much, behind them are the young people themselves, their voices, their lives."

Many children of all racial and ethnic backgrounds are joining gangs. Some become homeless, becoming a part of our downtown landscape. Many Black American youth are not making it in the educational system. The education system continues to fail them. In urban school systems all over the country, Black youth dropout rates are as high as 50%.

### What Is It Like To Be A Black Youth In America?

Young Black children face many obstacles. First, society ranks people of color, i.e., minorities, below Whites in America. Moreover, society differentiates among people of color, with Asians as the best (the model minority), then the Native American (the dying minority), then the Hispanic (the minority who is truly causing the browning of America), and, finally, Black people (the worst of the minorities, known as the drain on America).

The Black child is among the poorest people in America. He doesn't value life, because he has learned it is so easy to take. I believe this is a self-fulfilling prophecy. Society expects Black youth to be the gang member. The best recruitment tool for gangs is the media. Gangs get more free advertisements than any other industry in America, with the possible exception of community service announcements. The Black child is the drug addict, the pimp, and the pusher. I am as guilty as the rest of the world in terms of how I think about Black children. I cry one day, and criticize the next.

Digression: Often when I learn of a crime, I hope the perpetrator was not Black. I feel relief whenever the perpetrator is a White male or some other ethnic minority.

Black Americans face the challenge of starting at the bottom whenever they try to make it in America. The only exception is for top tier Black athletes, but these often end up sacrificing education for a few years of a high salary.

As a Black growing up in America, I like to think that I started out in the worst situation, but succeeded. I was a child in one of America's Black communities and yes, it was, and still is, labeled a ghetto community. Since my childhood, progress has been made – and lost – for Black youth. The government was my financial parent. Black youth had started to rise above that. But, with the dilution of affirmative action and welfare programs, Black youth are slipping back down again.

A Black kid always feels stress, because he or she has to endure other people's labels. For instance, people who are only a little better off financially will call a Black kid poor. I never knew I was poor until somebody told me so. Once I realized what this meant, I assumed the attitude of a poor person. A lot of my school-mates were poor, but they also did not realize it at that time, which was an odd blessing, as this label didn't rob them of their attitude and hope.

Fortunately for me, I grew up in a large family who supported me. My mother had six children, an average income of $400 a month, no husband, a boy friend who slept over from time to time, occasionally leaving ten to twenty dollars a week to support his kid. My mother was often sick with what was later diagnosed as mental illness, which eventually resulted in her death.

My father lived about five miles away. I saw him about once a week, as he drove by in his nice car. He always acknowledged me. Most of the time, he paid his alimony. My mother hauled him into court every year at Christmas to make him pay three months back alimony. That made Christmas not a bad time of the year. Receiving that little bit of money helped to make our lives easier around Christmas. In my late teen years, I went to live with my father and his schoolteacher wife. That was a very good thing. I feel fortunate that my stepmother accepted me as her own. She is still a wonderful role model for my children and me.

Most Black children do not share these same experiences. For many, their childhood is worse; for many, it is better. I believe my childhood was average for a kid growing up on the east bank of the Mississippi in New Orleans.

The missing element for many of America's Black youth is that their parents don't understand how to prepare them for formal educational. Many Black parents know that success in America comes through a good education. Every adult I knew as a youth told us we had better go to school and make something of ourselves. But, I never remember my parents making me do my homework, let alone helping me with my home work. I do remember them encouraging me to go to school. The key message was to get your high school diploma, which I almost didn't do.

The Black youth of today has to get this message. White America may have to help them get it. Blacks need one educated generation; the rest will follow. It happened for the Italians, Germans, and Swedes. It is now happening for the Russians and Romanians. Can you imagine the impact on America, if White Americans en masse decided to mentor Black youth? It goes without saying that the successful Black American adults should include mentoring Black youth as a part of their life mission. Many are doing just that.

Imagine being a young Black female in America. First, you have to learn to cope with the challenges young Black males face. The difference is that the Black female youth does not end up in the penal system, but society does expects she will be a financial burden to the government, specifically, to be pregnant by age 14 and on welfare. Young Black females are surrounded by the negative experiences of the Black male and his plight in America. Consequently, Black females often lose their hope of getting married and settling down to have families. Even if a Black female is educated and moves into middle class society, she may not marry. Social expectations are that she have children, but with the help of her mother, as my mother raised us with the help of her grandmother. Too often this message is prophetic.

Social expectations and labels help erode the self-esteem of Black youth. Based on social expectations alone, the outlook is bleak. Fortunately, I believe Americans are starting to dedicate themselves to saving the children of all races. We are starting to consider what is needed to get a Black kid out of the ghetto. Still undecided is who will pay for this solution and how. One thing is sure; the cost to save a child from the ghetto will increase the longer we take to act.

## *Can We Successfully Educate Our Black American Youth?*

I am convinced that the key to most of society's ills is education. All of us would live better, if we knew how to change the circumstances that quell our progress.

Nearly 11.5% of Black Americans are college educated, as compared to 25.2% of White Americans. In 1989, Black Americans earned 5.7% of all bachelor degrees. (Data source: Census 1990.) In my opinion, these statistics reflect America's priorities.

In 1997 and 1998, I was a school board member in Beaverton, Oregon. I was the only person of color on the school board. This was a very good thing. I was elected by a majority White vote, and my opponent was a White woman. I am the second person of color to sit on this board, but only a small portion of the school district's constituents are Black. My being there gave people of color a voice in the Beaverton education community. We spent a lot of time and effort on improving curriculum under the mission "success for all kids." Our labor was not in vain, because Beaverton kids did better on statewide testing than much of the rest of the state. The student body was approximately 80% White kids. The other 20% are kids of color and, of that most were Asian and Hispanic. During my tenure, I did not have the opportunity to actively research how well the Black students did compared to the White kids in Beaverton, but I kept listening for this information in this area. My suspicions were that most of the Black kids attending the Beaverton schools had well educated, middle class parents, since Beaverton is a fairly affluent community. However, most of the Black kids in the state of Oregon live in Portland, and attend Portland public schools. Overall, these kids are not as affluent as those in Beaverton, and don't have well educated parents to help them. Around 1996, many Black parents and leaders in the Portland community became frustrated over the poor academic performance of their kids. In particular, the kids had scored poorly in math and reading in statewide achievement tests for a number of years. They demanded that the superintendent do something to help their kids. The superintendent of the Portland School District, looking for some way to respond to the community, removed the entire administration and teaching staff from the poorest performing elementary school. This was the first time this much attention had been focused on a school that was failing Black American youth in Portland. As a result of this, there was evidence of academic improvement in the first year of the new administration.

It seems impossible to an educated Black American like me that this could happen in America. We have an education system that can educate one segment of the population and neglect another segment at the same time. We are successfully educating White kids, and Black kids beside them are failing. This is a problem that can be solved. The state of Texas is solving this problem by dedicating resources, time and money, and it is starting to work. One key piece of the solution is educating parents on the importance of their involvement in their kids' education.

We can educate our Black American children, and not only our Black American children, but all American children. The poor Black community is like a third world country within America when it comes to educating our children. We can help by holding these parents responsible for support at home. Like Texas, we need to spend the time and money on technology and develop a curriculum that will enhance the process. But, most important of all, we need to provide support and encouragement. I was a poor Black youth facing many of the obstacles that American Black youth face today. America helped me overcome them all.

### How Are Drugs Affecting Black American Youth?

The true plague for Black youth is drugs. There have been rumors that the CIA allowed drugs to come into the Black community of Los Angeles from foreign lands. The government is investigating these rumors. Although I have a hard time believing this, governments have done stranger things to benefit a group of people. Economic development in America is often seen as a zero-sum game, and it makes people do the strangest thing. Drugs are easy to get. A fast buck and addiction enable drugs to drive the economics of most urban ghetto communities.

Tobacco, alcohol, and other drugs continue to alter the minds of Black American youth, keeping them impoverished and addicted. Fortunately, drug use can be controlled.

### *What About Sex And Black American Youth?*

Too many of our young people learn about sex from the streets instead of their families. The too-frequent result is they have a warped sense of self-worth. As a society, we are adequately educating our youth about sex, at least those who attend schools. I hate holding schools accountable to educate our children in an area where family involvement, responsibility and values are so important. Nothing can substitute for parental involvement and guidance when it comes to areas of lifelong consequences. Requiring teachers to teach kids how they should develop and act in their relationships and in life is unfair to the teachers and to families. We all have different views and values about creating and living life.

Teenage pregnancy continues to rise. Adolescent parents have a hard time completing their education. Teen parents have difficulty finding work, and they have difficulty-finding daycare for their children. The result is a vicious downward spiral, which ends in more poverty. Guiding all children so that they don't get sucked into this downward spiral is important.

Interracial dating is becoming more and more accepted by White and Black Americans. Our youth are learning a lot about cross-cultural race relations. They are ignoring societal hang-ups and learning to get along. One possible consequence is that there may be more interracial marriages in the upcoming generation than in any preceding generation. I believe this to be a good thing!

**Chapter 14**

## *Will Black Youth Survive?*

America would not have it any other way. Many White Americans are now spending a lot of time trying to figure out what they need to do to help Black and all other American youth.

Black America is working hard to figure out what it needs to do to rescue the Black youth of America. Slowly, society is realizing that Black youth are a big part of America's future.

If you are reading this book around the year 2020, you are probably laughing. This problem was probably solved long ago, or is nearly solved. Just remember that I am probably still alive and, if I am, I care just as much about the youth of America as I did around 1998. I hope you care as much, and will do all you can to make this a great place for young Black people to live, work, and play.

# Chapter
# 15

## Chapter Fifteen - What Do Black Americans Think About Social Programs And Agencies?

*O*ne stereotype about Black Americans stands out from all the others, the myth that Black Americans love to be supported by the government. Most Black Americans become incensed when they hear White America say this. All of the Black Americans I know are so motivated to succeed that they overachieve at almost everything they do. The American assistance programs can be traps for the low income Black Americans by providing government assistance without guidance for the Black Americans to learn how to make it on their own. The government gives Black Americans bread, but doesn't teach them how, or give them the opportunity, to make the bread.

Social programs should always be a means to an end. As with many programs in America, they were started with the best of intentions. We often create solutions to problems, but we don't often go back to evaluate how well the solution works later, or determine if the nature of the problem has changed. If we do and find the solutions don't fit, we may get frustrated and want to scrap the whole program rather than alter it to fit better. As an engineer, I observed organizations tackle major technical problems in American business. Although we are good at improving gadgets and widgets, we struggle to find a better way to address social ills. Further confusing any social solution are our differences in race, culture, and beliefs that contribute to our different approaches.

We Americans often tangle ourselves in the very rope that we are trying to pull ourselves up with. However, we are also very good at repairing damaged ropes, and at replacing ropes that are worn out. Our social programs are the ropes. These ropes are vital to our existence in America. On the one hand, we need to improve our social planning. On the other hand, we are adept at helping communities to sustain themselves. To improve our effectiveness, community planning should reform and improve our social programs and tools. If we set our minds to do this, we will do it well.

### *For Whom Were These Programs Created?*

Most of the social service programs are disproportionately used by or applied to Black Americans, but they were originally created for White Americans. There are more White Americans on these programs than any other ethnic minority.

Social service programs have helped many Americans, but they have often crippled the same people when they try to improve their own economic station. In America, we often mistake privileges for rights. Because of this, people take advantage of social programs far longer than necessary. For example, many people who are able-bodied workers will stay on unemployment longer than they need to. I have had friends who went on vacation while they were on unemployment when a job was not only available but they were in the middle of being interviewed for it! Most of us don't think of unemployment as a social service program. Why? Because, we believe we earned it while we were working, and it is our right to draw unemployment. In my opinion, unemployment is just another subsistence program. The unemployment program was created in the 1930's with good intentions. At that time, it was used only as necessary and considered an embarrassment or shameful. But nowadays, many Americans believe it is their right to withdraw all of their benefits before getting another job. Most people are not poor and in the low income bracket when they first start to use unemployment. They may slip into the low-income bracket, if they don't take advantage of the programs placement benefit.

There are more low income Americans that are White than any other ethnic or racial group. But White Americans never lose access to the American dream. Using social service programs does not remove their opportunity to access the economic system. They are still susceptible to the same entanglements as other users of these programs, but their opportunities for economic advancement are far greater.

Although these programs were created for the White Americans, they became bad programs for Black Americans when many Black Americans learned to rely on them. An example is the stereotype of the Black welfare queen and she is a burden to society. Black Americans often enter these programs because of poverty, and the poverty-welfare legacy may get passed down through generations. In America, this should be unacceptable to any of us. Instead, we should ensure an equitable opportunity to everyone.

### Is Welfare Working?

The good news is government has revamped welfare (now called Aide to Families with Dependent Children, AFDC) so that it is an effective social and an economic development tool. In Oregon, the state government enhanced the welfare program, primarily to improve the lives of women. A work-training component was added to the financial subsistence. The success of Oregon's program is attested to by the fact that other states are using it as a model.

Despite its flaws, the old welfare program could be beneficial. As one who grew up in the welfare system, I am grateful that this country had such a program. For many years, I did not consider the program's mechanism or participants. I believe taking care of the poor is the least that we can do for this world. Welfare has been a means to an end for combating poverty in America. Black Americans have benefited from its provisions.

There will always be people who are needy and that means there will always be a need for charity in our society. Beside government assistance programs, there are private organizations' programs. Private charities can and have helped many people, and have, as a side benefit, reduced the welfare tax burden. Regardless of how the poor are helped, we should recognize our role as individuals to help them. In the Bible, Jesus is quoted as saying, "the poor you will have with you always." There will always be those who need help, and it is all of our right and privilege to take care them.

### *Is Affirmative Action Dying?*

Before addressing this issue, we need to understand the definition of the following terms:

**Affirmative** – (Webster) Affirming or asserting the truth, validity or fact of something. Positive, not negative. A manner or mode that indicates assent.

**Action** – (Webster) The process or state of acting or functioning; the state of being active. Something done or performed; act; deed. A practical, often organized activity.

**Affirmative Action** – (Webster) A policy to increase opportunities for women and minorities, especially in employment.

These definitions reflect that fact that Affirmative Action Programs were created with good intentions. President Johnson signed an executive order instructing the nation to do a better job of including all citizens in the opportunities afforded in the areas of government and business. He was ahead of his time.

Affirmative Action was policy and procedure for forcing America to include women and ethnic minorities, the majority of which were Black Americans, into the workforce. This program worked and was very successful. It achieved most of its objectives.

- It opened the doors for Americans of color to enter the workplace.
- It opened the doors for women to get into the workplace.
- It created programs to assist disadvantaged Americans to enter the higher education system and to help them be successful once they were in these educational institutions.

Affirmative Action provided numerous other benefits. White women benefited the most from this program. Although it is currently under attack, this program continues to benefit many of us. However, as of 1998, Affirmative Action as a government-sanctioned program is dying rapidly. Most states are ready to cancel its legislation and policy. Unfortunately, this successful program that has helped so many may die.

Affirmative Action may be one of those programs that gets scrapped before we realize how well it has worked. I am confident that we will put programs in place that will continue to help Americans be successful in the long run. We often break things and make matters worst before we realize how to make them better. I hope that we don't allow many of us to lose hope before we figure out how to restore the process. I have no problem with pushing out the old to bring in the new and improved, as long as we move quick and efficiently.

### *Are Black Americans Taking Advantage Of New Government Programs?*

Black Americans are often the last to be informed about new government programs, sometimes due to their own lack of interest. But, thanks to organizations like the National Urban

League and their ability to disseminate information and programs down to the community level, Black Americans are learning about these programs quickly. (I highlight the Urban League, because economic development for Black Americans is its priority, although it also provides services to other ethnic minorities and White Americans. It tries to bring its constituents and clients back into mainstream America as quickly as possible. The League's programs range from tutoring kids in K-12 to job training and placement for adults in all professions.)

The League is innovative in how it leverages one program to support another. One program helps senior citizens stay involved in the community by having them assist kids in the community. Although they are funded through numerous government grants, they are not afraid to leverage their resources by creating partnerships with the business community. Finally, the League chapters do a very good job of sharing their best practices with each other throughout the country.

### *Will Black Americans Continue To Need Government Help?*

The question is, will all Americans continue to need government help. Black people are now an integral part of American society and its economy. They, like all other Americans, have challenges, struggles, and successes. They will need the government as much as other Americans need the government. Black Americans have never been the leading cause for any of the government programs, except for those that fall under Civil Rights for Black America. We will need our government as much as our government will need us!

# Chapter
# 16

## Chapter Sixteen - Are There Things We Need to Know about Black Americans?

*I* want to share some secrets about Black Americans that are rarely revealed to a White American, unless you have a very close relationship with a Black American. As I stated in and earlier chapter, such a relationship might exist between college roommates and definitely would in an interracial marriage.

Black Americans have some unique characteristics that a lot of other races don't. Our hair is extra curly or, as we often say, "kinky." Kinky hair requires special treatment to be acceptable in America. Our skin is generally darker than that of any other race, except when we are products of interracial marriages, in which our skin tones may vary considerably. We also have different styles of greeting one another or talking to one another. These various characteristics make us unique as a race in America. Black Americans work very hard to stay unique. We often do so to preserve our cultural, but at other times we do this to be different from other Americans, especially White Americans.

### *How Do Black Women Care for Their Hair?*

Today, many Black women choose to process or treat their hair. The reason they do so is because commercials show beautiful, young, White women with straight, flowing, silky, smooth hair. These commercials have had an influence on Black Americans; young Black girls want straight hair. As a result, many Black women have their hair straightened. In the sixties and seventies, my mom would put a cast iron comb and a cast iron curling iron in an open flame and apply it to my sisters' heavily greased hair. My sisters screamed whenever a hot comb accidentally burned them. I always thought it seemed like a painful process. In this day and age, straightening is accomplished with very strong chemicals that relax the hair and is usually done by hairdressers who specialize in Black hair. When we were kids we use to tease the girls about how their hair was getting nappy if any water got on their heads. In New Orleans, where I grew up, the humidity was enough to turn heat-treated or chemically processed hair back to its natural state. I believe the chemical treatments have advanced enough that Black women don't have as much trouble keeping their hair straight as they did when I was a young kid in the sixties.

As a side note, There are a lot of hair care products that relax Black hair. However, Black hair care products are hard to find in stores like Kmart or Bi-mart. In contrast, most commercially advertised products are for White women, and these can be readily obtained almost anywhere.

In contrast to the straight hairstyle, there is a movement by some Black women to wear their hair in a natural style. Whoopie Goldberg not only wears her hair in a natural style, she wears it in a style that is African with a Caribbean influence called "dreadlocks." Natural Black hairstyles have been popular at other times as well. The Afro was in style during the late sixties and seventies, although it is not prevalent in the 1990's.

### How Do Black Men Groom Their Hair?

Most Black men have their hair cut at least once a month or more frequently. The most important aspect of cutting a Black man's hairs is to cut them evenly, because extra curly hair is sometimes hard to cut evenly. Once in Seattle, I needed my hair cut quickly. Since I couldn't find a Black barber, I went into a White barber instead. He was a nice gentleman who smiled and greeted me cordially and then explained to me that he was not experienced cutting Black hair. I told him, I needed him to cut my hair anyway, and I would tell him how to do it. He agreed to try, and we had fun. When he was done, he was quite proud of his first attempt. But that was exactly what I got, a first-attempt haircut. It was one of the most interesting haircuts I ever had. Although it looked bad by normal standards, I felt good I had given a new experience and education to a barber who had probably been cutting hair since before I was born. I believe he was glad for the opportunity. But, I don't think he ever advertised that he was an experienced barber for Black hair.

I remember when we young Black teenage men and thought it was fashionable to straighten our hair. You may remember the scene in Malcolm X when Denzel Washington and Spike Lee's characters are "conking their hair." Conk grease (I am not sure what the true chemical name is) will actually cause second and third degree burns on a person's scalp, if the residual is not washed away within 5-10 minutes. The scene in Malcolm X was hilarious when the two characters couldn't get water out of the tap to wash the grease out of Malcolm X's head. In this dire moment, he finds a creative solution – putting his head in the toilet! When Malcolm X becomes a Muslim, he cuts his hair very short into a style called an Ivy League hair cut. The Black Muslims of today still wear this hairstyle in order to have a well-groomed appearance. Unlike the straight hairstyle of Black women, this is definitely not the result of assimilation.

As of the late 1990's, many Black men have found it fashionable to shave their heads. So do White Americans. Movie stars and celebrates are considered sexy if they have cleanly shaven heads. Again, Black and White Americans prefer the same hairstyle, but now it is the no-hair hairstyle!

### *Is It True That A Large Percentage Of Black Men Do Not Shave With A Razor?*

Many Black American men have facial skin problems, due to the curliness of our hair. The name of the condition is called Foliculitis; we call it "hair bumps." This condition is a result of facial hairs curling under the skin and causing inflammation of the hair follicles. For the many Black men, shaving with a commercial razor is likely to cause these painful inflamed hair follicles. This condition can become worse by continuing to shave with a razor, resulting in a very sore and ugly face by American standards.

Most shaving commercials promote a smooth and close shave. They show a handsome White man whose clean-shaven face is being caressed by a beautiful White woman. The commercial promotes a razor that cuts hair beneath the skin for a really close shave. The electric razor takes it a step further by using two or three blades. The premise is the closer you shave, the more likely you are to get the girl, the prize or the job. (Hint, hint!) Black men feel totally ostracized by these commercials. The last thing you want is a shaver that cuts the hair off beneath the skin. If a Black man participates in this assimilation process, he will be in pain and agony when his facial hairs start to grow back. Rarely does a commercial promote shaving products for Black men. This is also a good example of how White-oriented the American media can be!

There is a solution to this problem that enables Black men to get a relatively close shave. It is called magic shaving powder, and it is a depilatory. It melts the hair at the skin line, and I believe it is one of the best products I have ever used. My face may not be quite as smooth as that White guy in the commercial, but I get a clean shave as opposed to a close one. This product is never advertised on the television. The only medium I have ever seen it advertised in is a magazine called "Ebony," a magazine that addresses Black readership. Most of the major drug store chains now carry this important cosmetic product. Although they don't sell a lot of it, I appreciate being able to get it when I need it.

# Do Black Americans Have Many Different Shades Of Skin Color?

Black Americans have many shades of skin color. Blacks with truly Black skin are rare in America, and they are generally foreign nationals who were born and raised in Africa. In America, we often refer to these people as being blue-black. Black Americans come in as many different shades of colors as all other ethnic groups combined. These shades encompass all hues found on the spectrum between White and Black Americans.

Since White Americans kept Black Americans as slaves the two races have mixed. Some historians explain that this mixing was a deliberate attempt to create lighter skinned offspring whose features were more like White features. Such offspring of White slave owners and Black women slaves would command higher market prices. Accordingly, these slave children were traded, sold as chattel property just as all the other slaves were.

In fact, there are Blacks of many different racial and ethnic ancestries. The most beautiful Americans, in my opinion, are those from mixed races. The Black movie stars of today are different shades of gray. (Pun intended.) Halle Berry, Vanessa Williams, Sinbad, Jada Pinkett and many others are products of mixed racial and ethnic heritages. But, as with slave days, America continues to prefer light-skinned Black American to the darker skinned one. There are exceptions. Wesley Snipes is a very successful Black actor that is relatively dark-skinned. Morgan Freeman and Samuel L. Jackson are fairly dark skinned, and have achieved a high level of success in the media. Denzel Washington is considered a brown-skinned Black American. Brown-skinned is an intermediate shade of Black.

The preference to light-skinned Black Americans can also be seen in government and business. Maynard Jackson and Andrew Young, both ex-mayors of Atlanta, are relatively light-skinned Black Americans. The late Reginald Lewis, the CEO of TLC Beatrice Corporation, was fairly light-skinned.

America's affinity toward light skin changes somewhat when in the area of sports. Darker skin athletes have a mystique of physical strength and ability. Sheer raw talent will, for the most part, transcend skin color. Michael Jordan is well received around the world, because of the great skill he possesses on the basketball court. The Nike Company has used his image to sell their goods for years. Some might say that Michael has helped sell more shoes to young Black kids than any other athlete in the world. I must admit, I have seen a lot of young White, Asian, Black, and every other color kid wearing Michael's face on a T-shirt. I don't think they care about his skin color. They simply know they have the greatest basketball player ever on their shirt, and so they must have the matching athletic shoes.

### *Are Blacks Americans Physically Stronger Than White Americans?*

Many White and Black Americans believe Black Americans are somehow stronger than White Americans. These thoughts may not be stereotypic thinking, as many people believe it is true. This is part of a great racial debate. I think the operative word is "opportunity." Many Black Americans have taken advantage of the opportunity to play sports. Many Whites see Black Americans performing in physically demanding and challenging sports. In football, Black Americans are usually the ball carriers and are seen running. This may be another self-fulfilling prophesy – America perceives Blacks as great athletes, and so affords them opportunities to become great athletes.

As a result of this, many White Americans believe Black Americans were somehow bred for sports. I have heard intelligent White educators state their opinions along the following lines: "Black Americans have their ethnic heritage in Africa. Their African ancestors had to run everywhere, so their legs evolved to enable them to become superior runners." There may be some truth to this, in that fast runners in Africa would have been more likely to survive, and have children who were fast runners. But, I know a lot of Black Americans who can't run very well, and do not like to run. And, I have seen many Black kids who are very slow runners.

Many of the Black athletes train their bodies to run, shoot, jump and all those other skills to play sports well. Because many Black Americans consider sports their only opportunity for advancement, they try their best to become top athletes. Likewise, White American athletes train their bodies to be as successful as possible. Interestingly in the area of football, White athletes play in most of the positions that require the greatest physical strength. Specifically, most down linemen are White athletes.

A number of factors contribute to the increasing number of prominent Black athletes. As more Black Americans are exposed to a greater variety sports, more of them emerge as top players in various sports fields. Black Americans highly value being very proficient at sports and sports are highly valued in our culture. That Blacks desire to be very good at sport may be a result of sheer determination to become successful through the set of opportunities that are available. Black parents often encourage children to play sports to win a scholarship to college. Most Black parents know they can't afford to send their kids to college and this is the chance for them to reach for the American dream.

### *Black People Seem To Enjoy Eating Fattening Foods, Why?*

The Black culture in America has created a style of preparing foods that is most delicious, but often unhealthy for the body. I have observed Black Americans in New Orleans, my hometown, truly enjoying some of the most fattening foods imaginable. Those foods that are stereotypically known as Black food are very delicious. Collard and mustard greens are usually smothered with ham hocks. Black Americans love rich sauces and gravies that are full of animal fats. We love to eat foods that are fried rather than baked. Our diets include vegetables that are over-cooked so that they lose their nutritional value.

Unfortunately, White Americans have also learned to love these fatty and richly prepared foods. This is part of the Black American culture that is being assimilated into the overall American culture. Anecdotal evidence of this is that almost every major national conference eventually ends up in New Orleans restaurants.

### Are Black Americans Less Physically Fit Than Other Americans?

Our diet and the lack of desire to exercise results in many Black Americans being overweight. I believe this is a part of the Black American culture. Joining fitness clubs is seen as an expensive luxury. Because many Black Americans believe they can't afford fitness clubs, they don't join. Many of my White friends are members of the local fitness center and exercise there several times a week. This is a regimen that Black Americans should adopt from the White American culture. I have noticed that Black Americans are starting to join health clubs as they become well educated and become part of the American middle class.

When I was in college, I spent a lot of time at the Intramural Athletic Center playing basketball and weight training. It is a part of the college campus culture to work out several times a week, and Black Americans that attend college adopt this practice. Similarly, most White Americans start to develop their own exercise regimens in college as well.

### Do Black Americans Have A Language They Call Their Own?

The answer to this question is no. As discussed earlier in the book, Black Americans have several unique dialects of the English language that they have created and find useful and fun.

When I was a kid, we used to speak in a variety of pig Latin that we had developed. I can't even remember any of the phrases. I do remember most words ended in "daka". If you wanted to say you, you said youdaka (pronounced "u-da-ka".) It was a cute language, and it lasted several years during high school.

Most Blacks have learned to manipulate English into something that sounds hip and cool. For instance, we might say, "what's up bra." This mean, what is going on in your life, brother? A reply to this might be "ain't nothin shakin this way." Translated this means, there is not much going on in my life. We Blacks often shorten words and phrases in the English language. We also have a lot of automatic responses. In the early seventies you agreed by saying "right on." Or we might say, "Yea man or so what!" (Whites who incorporate Black slang and Black idioms into their speech often make me laugh, because of their attempts to assimilate into the Black culture.)

Another trend is that some common Black slang has become part of everyday American lexicon. Jimmy Walker, the Black star in the sitcom "Good Times," made the phrases "what's up?" and "dyn-o-myte!" very popular. These became common household phrases in the early seventies. People still wear T-shirts with dyn-o-myte on the front.

One interesting characteristic of Black slang is that the meanings of pairs of words are often interchanged, sometimes so that they mean the opposite of the dictionary definition. For instance, if a Black teenager says, "That's a *bad* car," he doesn't mean it's a wreck. Instead, this use of "bad" means the car's looks are very appealing. Another example is, "that sister is cold." This could imply the female in question is hard to deal with or she looks beautiful and mysterious.

The Black dialect was created to be fun, not to fool anyone. I admit some of it comes from a misuse of the American grammar system. Ebonics is simply young Blacks trying to continue the traditions of their parents. Youth always puts its mark on what it touches, and Ebonics is a result of that youthful touch.

# Chapter 16

## *Why Do Black Americans Have These Ways and Things That They Think Are Exclusively Black?*

Blacks often feel a need to create things that make them different from Whites, because of the stumbling blocks that they encounter when going through the American assimilation process. That is, because they feel blocked, hindered, and cut-off from American culture, they choose to create, or enhance, their own culture.

Black ways and things should not make White Americans feel they are being excluded as a result of hatred. Black Americans would like to have you become part of their culture and world, just as they have attempt to become a part of your culture and world. This two way exchange is the only way we all come to the conclusion it is our world.

# Chapter
# 17

## Chapter Seventeen - Do Black Americans Have Access to the Political Structure In America?

*Y*es, Black Americans have access to the political structure of America, and they continue to make strides in helping to govern this country. But, we have a long way to go before we can count our political involvement as an area of major success. American politics, like American business, is based on economics, and economics is a contributing factor to inequity in America.

If the business world is the foundation for American success, then it is the political world that sustains American success and makes America tick. Why is a multimillionaire in business willing to set years of business accomplishments aside to pick up the mantle of politics? The answer has to do with wanting to have power and feeling patriotism.

Sidebar -Case in point: In the late 1990's, Bill Gates of Microsoft was hauled into court by the attorney general as part of an investigation into possible monopolistic behavior. At the time, Bill Gates was worth about $39 billion dollars, and Microsoft was worth over a $100 billion, depending on how the stock market was performing at any given moment. Perhaps you think that anybody with that much money could buy his or her way out of any kind of trouble. But this is not the case when an issue becomes highly charged politically. Many Americans believe the Microsoft investigation is all a matter of equity. The Attorney General threatened Gates and Microsoft with fines of $1 million dollars a day, if Microsoft did not stop including Microsoft Internet Explorer

Browser, software used to search for information on the internet, in a bundle of software sold to computer manufacturers. At issue was that Microsoft included this software at no extra cost, in order to gain market share. Naturally, the computer manufacturers would not likely include a competitor's Internet browser software that they need to pay for. Microsoft's competitors in the area of Internet browsers claimed this was monopolistic behavior. Software developers of other products also complained that Microsoft was becoming a monopoly. None of those vendors had the power to challenge Microsoft individually. So, they went home and told their mother, the U.S. Government, that Microsoft wasn't playing fair. Mom, or The U.S. Attorney General, took up the challenge to protect her smaller children from being bullied by one of her bigger children. The point of this example is that power in America does not come from wealth alone. In fact, political power is greater than business power.End Sidebar

The political system in America is the most powerful in the world. It regulates nearly about everything we do, use, buy, sell, or borrow. At the same time, this system allows us to accomplish many wonderful things that make us proud to be an American. There is no other government that is as successful as we are at this point in history. There is no other country where people are so happy just to arrive here and taste freedom. Black Americans are as proud of this system as other Americans.

Politics, like other American systems, discriminates based on skin color. Black Americans have a different set of opportunities than White Americans do. Sometimes these opportunities are separate but equal but separate, which in most cases makes them inequitable. White Americans have a hard time understanding these inequities, perhaps because they face their own challenges when they attempt to access these opportunities. Often, they don't often understand that if they find the process to be difficult, it is twice as difficult for Black Americans.

The U.S. government has acted like a mother to all its citizens. But as those of us who are parents know, sometimes it is hard not to show favoritism. Understanding the different needs of children is one of the biggest challenges a parent faces. Similarly the American government tries to treat all its citizens alike, even if some have different needs. This cookie-cutter approach can result in treating some people unfairly.

### *How Has Black Americans Fared In Politics Lately?*

In spite of the shortcomings of the political system, it has treated Black Americans more fairly than any other system in America. Affirmative Action and the Civil Rights bill are evidence of this. Black Americans have gained a higher percentage of government jobs than they have gained in corporate America, because of successful political races and appointments. They have also made strides, wherever economic success, or large campaign troughs, have not been necessary for political success. Black Americanscontinue tomake great strides in local governments, including becoming city council members, mayors, and other types of political administrators.

City and local municipalities where Black Americans are a major part of the demographic makeup have very good Black representation in leadership. More cities are electing Black mayors and council members. This, in turn, has led to more Blacks in administrative management positions, such as executive aides and city managers. These key positions in society have enabled Blacks to make great strides in the world of local governments. An important milestone is the influence Black politicians have over the way local taxes are spent. Each success makes it a little easier for future Black politicians to succeed.

However, White Americans have started to scrutinize the political system since Black Americans have started to gain access to this type of American power. White Americans have attacked the way political district boundaries were drawn that resulted in African Americans winning seats in their state legislature and senates. African Americans are far from parity representation in those law-making bodies. As a result of these challenges in the late nineties, Black Americans are starting to lose ground at the national level.

In the nineties, there were some successes and some losses. Carolyn Mosley-Braun was the first Black American to become a Senator. Many candidates from organizations such as the National Congressional Black Caucus lost campaigns for seats in the U.S. Congress. With the upcoming elections, there will be another set of national leaders. Hopefully, it will use its power to remedy some of our social ills.

### *How Many Black Americans Are In the Senate, Congress And Other Powerful Elected Offices?*

The answer is short. In the nineties, there is one Black Senator and one Black representative in the House at the national level.

### *Does The Democratic Party Still Appeal To Black Americans?*

Black Americans are endeared to the Democratic Party. John F. Kennedy convinced Black America that the Government and the Democratic Party really cared about them. However, it was not Kennedy who implemented most of the successful Affirmative Action programs, but Lyndon B. Johnson. Johnson should get the credit. Kennedy was the president who started drawing the country's attention to Black American issues and needs.

In the late nineties, President William Clinton named more Black Americans to high level political appointments than had been named before. Some of those positions included the first Secretary of Commerce Ron Brown, who died in a plane crash in the line of duty, and the first African American Secretary of Energy, Hazel O'Leary. He also named an African American as the Secretary of Agriculture, and many other people of color to high level jobs in the White House. For Black Americans, he was the most progressive president they have ever experienced. His administration also had the honor of a having a healthy economy for many of the years he was in office.

The Democratic Party continues to be more liberal than the Republican Party. It sponsors more socially oriented bills. Whether you think that liberalism is good or bad for the country, African Americans usually benefit from the social bills this party sponsors. Furthermore, the Democratic Party is usually more supportive of ethnic, minority and political candidates. There are more Black American Democrats than there are Black American Republicans.

### *Are There Black American Republicans?*

Blacks were loyal to the Republican Party, because Abraham Lincoln established the Emancipation Proclamation to abolish slavery and started the Civil War to enforce it. The Republican Party has changed a lot from its ultra-conservative stand in the 60's and 70's to a more moderate political organization under Ronald Reagan and George Bush. As Black Americans obtaining college degrees, more have become more astute in politics. Consequently, many Black Americans have started to look for a choice in political parties. Many of today's Black Americans have elected a more conservative approach to government and chose to become part of the Republican Party. Many Black Americans do not realize how conservative they really are as a result of their religious beliefs, specifically many have taken pro-life and anti-abortion stands. In addition, many Black Americans realize how much government interferes in their lives in the name of helping them.

Some of the rising stars and leaders, such as, the Reverend J.C. Watts have chosen to represent the Republican Party. J.C. Watts has a strong backing in the Black American community. In my opinion, he appears to be very successful in articulating a political agenda that is very progressive for Black America. Many

Black leaders seem to trust him and support him. However, often the Black community will not embrace a Black candidate if they choose the Republican Party.

The Republican Party, like the rest of society, is starting to reach beyond its Eurocentric views of the world and realizing that it has to embrace a diverse culture. In this regard, it is following corporate America. I think this has been very good for Black America, for the country, and for the Republican Party. But, progress is not an end result, and the Republican Party has a lot to learn to successfully embrace an increasingly diverse society.

### Can A Black American Ever Be President Of The United States?

Is America ready for a Black President? I believe the country is becoming ready for a Black president. Americans seemed to demonstrate that feeling when they attempted to adopt Colin Powell as a presidential candidate. I am not sure General Powell would have been elected, but he would have given any opponent a run for the money. I definitely believe General Powell could have raised the money needed to run a well-funded campaign. He clearly gave the Republican Party a boost as the first African American to keynote a Republican Electorate Convention.

General Powell has all the right stuff to be President of the United States. He has paid the dues required to hold the most powerful political position in the world. He was National Security Advisor, and held the position of chair of the Joint Chiefs of Staff. No other Black American has ever climbed that high in our political system.

Would he be a good president? I believe so, and so do many White Americans. Will he run in the future? I believe his family has said no, and I believe he will honor them.

Reverend Jessie Jackson was the first Black American to seriously attempt to raise the money to run for the highest office in the land. He never had a chance, but he made Black America realize it could come to the table and play in this game. I believe he set the stage for a J.C. Watts or some other hopeful who is developing in the wings. He has also made himself a respectable unofficial U.S. ambassador to the third world. No one appears to be able to stop him from conducting diplomacy in the name of peace. This type of success demands great respect, and he deserves it. I may not be a great fan of Jessie, but I do respect him. Jesse Jackson also has significant clout with corporate America. They consider him an affirmative action and diversity police, but there is very little they can do to stop him. As soon as he smells a discriminatory practice, he revs up his political machine, and off he goes. Reverend Jackson does not always know exactly what to do, but his intentions are usually to make White Corporate America be fair to Black America.

He continues to be in the political "thick of things" when he deems it necessary. He continues to have a strong voice on Capitol Hill. The politicians may not want to listen to him, but they do. That has to be good for Black Americans, as well as for all Americans.

### *Is White America Ready For A Black American President?*

White America is ready for a Black President. I believe a woman may become president before a Black American does. This woman could possibly be Black, but more than likely will be White. I do find it interesting that big screen media is portraying Black American men in presidential role. The two instances that I viewed this in 1997 and 1998 were both disaster films where the presidents were in control of the country, but not totally in control of the situation. Those two films were the "Fifth Element," a futuristic comedy, staring Bruce Willis, and "Meteor" staring Morgan Freeman as president.

I believe the Black American who becomes president will live in great fear. There is still a large body of White Americans who believe White is supreme in America. This is not just a bunch of fanatics. These are blue-blooded Eurocentric Americans who own a piece of this rock, and don't want to yield control to anyone who does not look like them. These people may try kill or incapacitate a Black president, just because he or she is Black.

I believe that there are Black Americans who are quite capable of running this country. I believe America is rapidly becoming aware of all of its resources, including the assets it has in Black America. I believe that Black leadership at all levels is ready to explode and assume its rightful place in America. We have earned it, and we want to keep having the opportunity to earn more!

# Chapter
# 18

## Chapter Eighteen - Does the Black Church Play a Major Role in America?

*T*he Church is the largest and oldest and most segregated institution in America. There is truly a White Church and a Black Church. The Black Church has become one of the most powerful entities in America. Furthermore, it continues to gain political, economical, social, and spiritual power. Although many Americans have fallen away from what they often term as organized religion, "The Church" is still the backbone of our belief system. This is relevant to this discussion, because belief systems are very important in the assimilation process. Therefore, the church is an important tool for the assimilation of Black Americans into mainstream America.

The church contributes to the American culture in many ways. It provides a network of affiliated organizations that people trust overall, even though there are newsworthy exceptions. It fills a role that we don't allow government, business, or our families to fill specifically providing moral standards and accountability. Americans don't like to relinquish control to any organization devoid of a cohesive and thorough mission and belief system. We, therefore, are willing to relinquish some control over the moral and spiritual aspects of our lives to the church. The church holds the arguably unique role in American society as an institute of moral accountability, a place to preserve our traditions, and a spiritual center that generates hope. Taking these factors together, the church is first and foremost a stabilizing force in the American culture and more than performs those duties for Black Americans.

The church provides a system of accountability. Most people believe they, and others, should be held accountable. We have a hard time agreeing on what should and should not be a part of that accountability system. This dissention is part of the reason there are so many church denominations. Although many of us like the idea of having moral standards, fewer of us like to have our short-comings with regard to these standards pointed out. Many of us don't like someone checking up on our church attendance, and, even less, our behavior outside of church. Although many of us want a moral standard as a social backbone, we personally resent being compared to that standard. Black American are no different than other Americans when it comes to these measurements.

The church is a place to preserve our traditions and re-instill them with meaning. We Americans are very steep in tradition and we like to keep tradition in our societal structures, families and homes, and other secret and safe places of sanctuary. The church has been a sanctuary both spiritual and physical for Black Americans since antebellum times. Today, traditions are hard to keep in our families without an entity like the church that transcends generations and geography. None of us could retain the vast knowledge of information and history necessary to maintain traditions, but the church can. Frequently, these traditions are related to practices that we no longer observe, but we like the idea that they are not forgotten. Black Americans love to honor these traditions kept as treasures by the church.

The church also retains beliefs and attitudes that we hold dear and sacred. Although we may be willing to die or kill for these beliefs, we may have a hard time living lives that are true to them. The institution of the church is where we learn and are reminded of these beliefs and practices that we have such a hard time including in our everyday lives. Black Americans cling to many good beliefs that the church has fostered. These beliefs have allowed them to persevere through some tough times down through the years. One belief that the church has fostered is the belief in patriarchal leadership.

The church is a place to seek guidance. In the Black church, the spiritual leader is practically always a man; he is expected to provide guidance to the church's members. Usually, this leader relies on a small group of other men, perhaps elders or deacons, to discuss ideas and help govern or manage the church members. Sometimes these groups are selected through quasi-democratic processes, but, in reality, the church leader generally handpicks the men in this group. In the Black American church, this church leader is usually a very fatherly figure, and one of his primary roles is to surrogate fatherhood to the church members. If the church leader does not have a strong enough personality, some of the women in the church will probably carve out an unofficial position for themselves as the church matriarchs. Generally, these women do a wonderful job helping to run the operations of the church, just as they have learned to run single-family households. Therefore, the Black church's social structure reflects the social structure of the Black American family.

Many Black Americans turn to the church for hope, sympathy, and pity. We are not afraid to bare our soles and emotions in church. Music and sermons in Black churches reflect the deep feelings of the members, as well as encourage them to express these feelings. In contrast, White Americans are generally more, emotionally restrained in church, but they, too, are more open with their feelings in church.

The church has played am important role in helping Black Americans endure difficulties and finding hope. Whenever Black Americans have felt hopelessness and despair as a result of the inequities in American society, the church has brought them through the hardship. The more Black Americans are persecuted, the more they turn to their church and their God. Their church always provides the leadership they need to get through their trial. Southern Black Americans have experienced terrible troubles for years, but the church carried them through. Even when the Black Church itself comes under fire, it still provides a call to reason and reconciliation.

Finally, the church is the ultimate support group for most of us. All my human "things and stuff" I have to deal with in life have been previously considered by church doctrine and teaching. I can turn to that teaching to help me sort things out. Perhaps, this is true for me in both the Black and White churchesI have attended. But Black people in general have closer emotional and community ties to their church, and, therefore, not only value the church as a support group for the individual, but for the whole community. Walking down the street in the Black community you might hear a minister encouraging the local yokel to come to church.

Based on the information above, it is clear why Black people would look to the church for hope, guidance, moral structure, and support. The church has been the backbone of Black America, and continues to give strength to the Black American struggle. The church continues to produce leaders and to provide the sane voice that keeps America out of civil unrest.

### *What Are Some Of The Attributes Of The Black Church As Compared To The White Church?*

There are many differences in the content of Black church services as compared White church services. The music is much more upbeat and has more of a jazzy, soulful feel and sound. We Black people don't just sing, we clap and pat our feet and bellow out the words to sacred hymns. Many of the new evangelical White church movements are copying some of the musical styles of Black church services. The Black congregation is much more interactive with the speaker. They are known to encourage a speaker by yelling out amen all through out the ministerial message. Most White church member sit quietly and meditate on what the speaker is saying. Black churches are more apt to set aside parts of the service for focusing on healing, prayer, foot washing and long bouts of singing, praise and worship. This leads to longer services as compared to the White church. Proportionately there appear to be many more Black churches than White churches per capita especially in the south. We use to say, there is a church and a liquor store on every corner of Algiers (in New Orleans).

I believe the Black church has more status and power over what happens in a Black community than White churches have in White communities. The minister is always visible to the community and is usually very vocal in local politics and other community matters.

Most of the denominations of Black Churches in the south are off shoots from the Southern Baptist. The African Methodist Church is a up and coming denomination and is known as the AME Church. The AME church is thought to be a relatively new power force in the community. I have never seen a Black Presbyterian Church. There are numerous types of holiness churches and some of them have church services that last 5 to 6 hours.

### *Are Black Americans Really More Religious than White Americans?*

Yes, I believe this to be true, but, with that answer, I need to define the word "religious." Religious may be defined as:

- A belief in God and practicing the traditions that go with that belief.
- Not merely practicing traditions, but basing one's entire existence in a belief that practicing these traditions will enable me to endure whatever bad things come along.
- A demonstration of beliefs through sincere outward emotional display.

In light of this definition, Blacks could be perceived as more religious than Whites in America. Because of the persecution Black Americans have suffered, they have turned to the church. The church has provided Black Americans with sympathy and hope.

Black Americans have learned to seek the church as a source of hope and a social role model from the time they are small children. Black children are brought to church by their parents, aunts and uncles, or whomever was the family relative raising them. These children learn that the church is the safest place in America. They believe it is fairly free of White influence. They see Black American men in leadership positions. (For many years, Black children only saw Black adults in leadership positions as church leaders and teachers.) Black children believe what they hear in church to be the ultimate truth. They see the people in the church as having authority over all other authority figures in their lives, with the exception of their parents.

I remember attending church with my mother, aunts, and grandparents. Most of my family members were members of the leadership structure. I had an uncle who was the pastor until he died. I had a cousin who was a minister as long as I can remember, and she was very faithful. My grandfather was a well-accomplished singer, and could lift our congregation to incredible emotional heights. Through these services, I encountered the greatest power I ever remember as a child. I will never forget the songs and stories of my early childhood. Even today, they give me great comfort.

When my life is not going well, I recall those days of safety and comfort. I consider myself a religious person, and I find that most of my comfort comes from my belief in God and his ability to affect my life negatively or positively. My belief in God brings me happiness and joy, even during times of trouble. This gives me insight into how a people can survive the many atrocities such as those Black Americans survived the last three hundred years. I am also grateful for the progress Black Americans have made in the last fifty years. Because of this progress, I am grateful for my life in America. There are very few other things that have the kind of power in my life that my belief in God has.

### *What Is The Makeup Of The Black American Church?*

Today a large proportion of people who attend Black churches are women and children. Many of these women are single, divorced, or unaccompanied by their husbands. These women give

White Americans the perception that Black Americans are more religious than White Americans are. They ensure the survival of the Black church. Moreover, these women also provide the Black American church with strength that seems to have no end when adversity strikes.

Digression: I don't believe that individual Black Americans face more adversity than individual White Americans do. There are a lot of socially poor White Americans who experience social economic depression just like many Black Americans. But the difference is that these White Americans can hope for the opportunities that are available to White America. I believe that Black Americans as a people suffer adversity, because of the way America is constructed socially. Black Americans in general are still dealing with social and economical adversity.

Black women, in my opinion, use the format of the church to allow Black men to gain and practice leadership skills. In contrast, White men learn how to become strong leaders in the business world. The only other venue for Black men to gain and practice leadership skills is in sports. Unfortunately, leadership skills gained in sports are not as transferable as those gained in the church and business world.

As we explained earlier, the pastors and top church leadership of the church are Black men. The rest of the church leaders are women, including Sunday school superintendents, the treasurers, the secretaries, and teachers. Black women accomplish most of the work of the church. What has baffled me as a Black man is the ability of these women to put the support structure in place to foster an environment where Black men can learn and grow. This environment is a place where many Black men have learned what dignity is. It is a place that allows the men to build their self-esteem and confidence by learning how to speak to large groups of people. Significantly, this is where most of Black politicians first learn to address groups, summarize problems, and state conclusions.

### *What Does The Black Church Offer To The Economics Of Black Americans?*

In the last twenty years the Black Church has led the charge for the economic development of Black Americans. It has lobbied the government; it has written grants for inner city development, and continues to create community development entities that increase the wealth of Black Americans.

The church is starting to teach Black Americans about investing and saving for retirement and economic growth. Many churches have encouraged their congregations to start investment clubs to take advantage of their corporate investment benefits. This information allows Black Americans to take advantage of benefits made available to them through corporate America.

Although the Black church encourages its congregations to invest in, i.e., do business within, its own communities, there is still a lot of room to build a stronger Black economy within a local community. Black Americans still have a hard time doing business in their own communities. This is a catch twenty two. Local communities lack resources to provide all the goods and services its residents want, resulting in the residents doing business outside the local communities. Because of relatively low sales volumes, local businesses have lower capitalization and a general lack of resources. Black Americans are just learning to pool their resources to strengthen their buying power. Such power can create the wealth, or capital, needed to start local business, which, in turn, will fuel a community's economic engine.

Single-handed, the Black church is empowering Black Americans and providing them with the skills to become employed and to stay employed. Many Black churches in the eastern United States have their own employment programs or have teamed with other community partners to create and sustain valuable employment programs. Many of the Urban Leagues in America look to local pastors to help implement their programs and to find job candidates.

## *What Affect Does Burning Black Churches Have On Black Americans?*

As of the late nineties, the latest persecution and trial that Black Americans are facing is the burning of their churches. Please do not read this section without reading the entire chapter or you won't get the full effect of the information. Previously, I explained what the Black Church means to Black Americans and the way Black Churches contribute to Black communities. Because of the importance of the church to Black communities,church burnings are devastating to Black Americans.

Churches are the hearts of Black people's communities and faith. When a Black church is burned, its members hope and existence are threatened. This destroying the ethnicity of a culture that gives a people their distinctiveness and creativity. The burning of Black churches says we not only want to destroy you, we want to punish and torture you. We don't want you to find any comfort in your existence. We dare to attack your belief in God.

The single most successful system that Black Americans have established in America is the Black church and burning it is attacking the hope that lies with in them. History has proven time and time again, you will devastate and decimate a people if you attack and destroy their belief system. You will then relegate them to dependence and subservience. These people will have very little to live for and will fight to the death trying to defend it and will destroy everything in the process. The Black church is a big part of the solution in making America work for Black and White Americans.

# Chapter 18

## *How Has The Black Church Affected The Rest Of America?*

It is easy to see that the Black church has many times come to the rescue of America. During slavery it saved many lives and kept slaves from revolting. Many ministers taught their congregations to work hard for their masters and that God would eventually deliver them from their suffering and pain. It provided the little bit of joy that slaves experienced while they were being treated as animals.

The Black church was one of the first institutes of learning and created the first historic black colleges, which continue to educate many young Black Americans today. It continues to assist, encourage and honor Black youth that strive to complete their college education.

As we stated earlier, it is the training ground for many Black leaders and politicians. Martin Luther King Jr. learned to lead in the church and became a great pastor, minister and leader of Black America. He led America into this tolerable era we entered during the 60's. His children have continued to use the church as the springboard for great leadership. His daughter is a minister and seems to be following in her father's footsteps.

The Black church continues to create many of the top entertainers of today. Aretha Franklin, Dione Warwick, Stevie Wonder perfected their talents under the watchful eyes of their pastors and church choir directors. Divas Whitney Houston and Brandy are the latest sensations to perfect their crafts in the Black Church and are now second generation.

America should treasure the Black church it has kept us from civil unrest many times in the history of America. It continues to be the calming voice in the Black community during any of today's unrest due to the ills that still plague our society because Black and White Americans still don't have a full understanding of each other. There are times when the entire American church is working and praying together and the results are extremely powerful.

I truly believe it will be the church of America that heals this land from racial unrest and injustice. It will be the church that will prevail once again in our history. It has always and will always be the rod of reason in America.

# Chapter
# 19

## Chapter Nineteen - Tearing Down The Walls Of Enmity: Is This The Solution To Our Problems?

$W$e Americans have created solutions to every problem we have encountered. We continue to solve the problems of the world, but, like most families, we tend to ignore our members that live at home with us. Similarly, we ignore the homeless in America and send money to other countries in the name of good foreign policy. I would like to predict that in the *21st* century, we will not only see a cure for cancer, heart disease, and many other diseases that plague us, but we will also turn our attention to fixing our people systems. Yes, I am an eternal optimist, but I believe I live in a country that loves its people more than anything else and it will honor that love soon.

The walls that have been built between White and Black Americans over the last two hundred years are the last walls in our society to come down. These walls are rooted in the covert racism that continues to plague every system in America. Racism is curable, but we need to develop a focus to remove it from our societal systems. There are many solutions at work today repealing racism on a daily basis. As a result, I see racism losing its hold on America. One of the first solutions to destroying the wall of enmity is the exchange of information and communications.

## Can Black and White Americans Communicate with Each Other?

America has perfected its ability to communicate. In the age of technology-assisted information exchange, we are making large strides in our ability to communicate. Even the media holds conversation of how diverse we are in America. The news media includes Black Americans in its coverage. As I talked about in an earlier chapter, many Black Americans are being seen on the big screen as stars in blockbuster movies. There is still Blackploitation, but we are starting to see Black Americans in leadership positions. Often, these leadership roles are in the military, but this is reflective of a trend in society. The military has been most successful at providing opportunities for many Black, as well as all, Americans.

In 1989, I moved to Boise Idaho. One of my first Boisean experiences was being interviewed by the local newspaper, in which I was a voice for Black America concerning the image of Idaho. The newspaper reporter followed me to Anaheim, California to observe me and others interviewing young Black Engineering students for summer internships. This type of media inclusion helps to increase inclusion in society and gives Black America a stronger voice where they were thought to be silent. White Americans in Idaho read how Black Americans from all around the country view Idaho.

While on my recruiting assignment most of the young Black American engineering students I encountered initially thought of Boise as Hicksville and Potatoland. They believed that Boise did not welcome Black Americans living in their midst. In the job interviews, I shared my initial opinion of Boise, which was very positive. I told the job candidates about the job opportunities offered by international hi-tech companies that have settled there. After hearing from a fellow Black American that their impression of Idaho was incorrect, they were more open to considering Boise as a place to have a summer work experience. One of the factors that had influenced the candidates' impression were the media reports of Idaho as the home of the Aryan Nation, with a number of members in Cour de Lane. Boise is over 400 hundred miles away from Cour de Lane, and is inhabited by former Californians who have fled the high cost of housing and crowds in California. Many young Black Americans come to Boise for summer and to accept permanent jobs. But, I am sad to report, they usually stay an average of two to three years, before they move to larger metropolitan areas with higher populations of Black Americans. Boise lacks the role models they need to further develop their careers.

### *Who Are The Role Models For Black America?*

Another effective method to tear down this wall is role modeling. Role models are people who help other people obtain appropriate knowledge and experience that lead them to successfully attain social goals. Examples of role models include corporate champions, passionate teachers, and entire families who will take a non-family member into their homes. These role models are willing to sacrifice some of their comforts to help others gain an education and set of experiences they couldn't otherwise get.

Most Black Americans want to reject the real answer to the question of who are our role models. But although we reject it, the answer is often White Americans. We want to reject this answer, because we have only been allowed to emulate White America for the last 30-40 years. Even as we continue to reject it, we continue to accept the inevitable. Once a people become a part of a society, they will be pressed into its processes, especially the assimilation process. White Americans have modeled all of the most important experiences that Black Americans have needed for many years. A typical example is White Americans who not only hire Black Americans, but who develop Black Americans once they are on the job. I have benefited personally from good role modeling from White Americans that helped me gain some of the experiences that led to my successes in the business world.

### *Can We Apply Inference Thinking To These Problems?*

What is inference thinking? Inference thinking uses knowledge gained from experiences to infer connections or solutions in a logical fashion. It is a way to define, analyze, and solve the most complex of problems. Inference thinking is not unique to Americans, but the way we apply it is.

However, the approach usually used in addressing racial problems is interpolative thinking. Interpolating is altering, modifying, or filling in information that is missing. The assimilation process breaks down when interpolative thinking influences social systems. As Americans, we sometimes fall into the trap of using interpolative methods to understand data, and end up misguided and frustrated. An example is how Black youth in America continue to struggle with crime, drugs, and the punitive systems. Using interpolative analysis we have concluded that we should build more jails and increase the size of our police forces. In other words, we observe what is happening and, instead of applying logical thinking to reach the best solution or to try to better understand the problem, we jump to a conclusion. Not only do White Americans sometime use interpolative thinking to derive solutions to problems, but Black Americans sometimes use interpolative thinking to interpret their relationships with White Americans.

In contrast, by using inference thinking, we examine the information we have and analyze it in light of our goals and priorities. An example of inference thinking is having engineers design a defect-free production process that will produce products that are defect-free. The engineers don't focus on defective products, but the process, to achieve the desired results. (One corporate slogan captures this thought concisely, "Design in Quality.") Deming was the innovative thinker who applied inference thinking to manufacturing. Thomas Watson and Bill Gates have applied it to information systems. With respect to Black youth, our goals are to develop them into well-educated adults who contribute to their communities and have high quality of life. By bringing the proper resources, education and technology to Black youth, we can derive these desired results. We are more than capable of doing this! We do this every day in our American corporations and businesses. The high quality work teams that we are deploying in our businesses and corporations are tremendously successful in applying inference thinking. The military has been very successful at designing good development programs for Americans of all color, and they get the planned results. There are few unsuccessful people in the military, which can be largely attributed to the military's continuously refining its program to train our military personnel. The military example points out how inference thinking and Deming quality processes can be applied successfully to developing people.

### *Do We Have A Secret Weapon In Our Social Arsenal Called Education?*

One key factor to "Designing in Quality" for our Black youth is education. I have experienced both poor education hindering progress and good education boosting progress. Being from New Orleans, Louisiana (or as it has been referred to by those in the know, Lousy Anna), I have experienced the worst public education system in the USA. It competes with Mississippi for the honor as the worst system in America; the two states teeter back and forth as to whom gets the badge of shame. Louisiana and Mississippi have very large Black American populations. I remember finishing high school with my 2.3 GPA and thinking I had accomplished something. Well I had, it just wasn't enough to take me anywhere. Upon arriving at the University of Washington after a military career, I was devastated to find out I couldn't compete on par with my fellow White students. I won't bore you with the details of how I was given the opportunity to develop and did catch up. Plain OLE' American Opportunity came to the rescue in the form of an Equal Opportunity Program (EOP). This program included remedial training, study halls and tutoring. Only in America could I have risen from the ashes of the Louisiana education system to the halls of the University of Washington and graduate in the top half of my class.

Again, opportunity is the secret to bringing White and Black America together. I now lead problem-solving sessions in corporate America, on government committees, and as the superintendent of Sunday School for a 2000 member, mostly White American church. Getting Black America educated along with White America is a true solution. This is already work in progress. As Black America continues to progress into the American middle class. The walls between White and Black America continue to erode. Black Americans still need to make up a lot of ground, but it is true progress.

### *Should White Americans Take Time To Study Black Americans?*

Black Americans have studied White Americans out of necessity. Until a hundred years ago, White Americans owned all the sources of income in America, and Black Americans had to know what these White American owners and managers were about in order to work for them. Today, White Americans continue to control the economic opportunities for America. Black America still finds it important and necessary to understand what White Americans care about and how they think. Similarly, White American workers study their White bosses out of necessity. But, because Black Americans don't wield most of the economic control in America, White Americans don't find a need to learn much about Black Americans.

This imbalance will continue for many decades, but now is the time for the process to become more balanced with Black and White Americans both trying to understand each other. White Americans should look at the stereotypes present in today's American culture and start to study how Black Americans think. The more time you put into this study, the more you will get out of it. For example, one of my White American female students made it clear that she was skeptical about what the class could teach her about the human race. She was inexperienced with people of color and had taken the class out of curiosity. To make this story short, near the end of the class she shared with me how understanding more about people of color had erased some of her fears away and helped her communicate with people of color, especially with Black people. She told me she was now dating a Black American. I could tell she was experimenting with her new knowledge. I warned her to be careful, and take it slow. She ended up struggling with the relationship, due to her lack of understanding of Black Americans. She also chose a guy who ended up taking advantage of her curiosity and took advantage of her naivete. Later in the year, she wrote me an e-mail to tell me the relationship wasn't working, but she was okay. It was an interesting case study for both of us.

This is the kind of relational interaction that has to continue to take place. I must admit that some of this is experimental. But then, many of our problems are solved through experimenting, specifically by daring to develop relationships. Relationships between Blacks and Whites do not have to be romantic. They can be work relationships, organizational relationships and, most importantly, friendships. Remember that the benefits on a personal and societal level will outweigh the risks.

### *Is Affirmative Action Still A Viable Solution?*

Affirmative Action as a tool will remain controversial as long as there is not another tool designed to replace it. America likes to obsolete technology, systems and programs long before they are no longer useful or being used. Affirmative Action is a program that many White Americans feel is out-dated and not helpful. White Americans continue to feel it is unfair to today's young White American males. And, they are right. But, they fail to remember how unfair and how long Racism has continued to plague Black

Americans. And, they may have failed to recognize that White American women were the biggest beneficiaries of Affirmative Action.

Affirmative Action has an element of reverse discrimination. If one group of people has discriminated against another for a hundred years, how long will it take to reverse this discrimination and its effects? How long before those who once discriminated start to feel that they are now the objects of discrimination? Therefore, why are we afraid to say to a young White guy that you didn't get the job because we have disproportionately fewer women and minority engineers in this company than in our community? Why can't we say that finding this balance was one of our recruiting criteria and business objectives? We still have serious inequities in America where race and gender are of concern. Black Americans will continue to demand that we be allowed to participate in the benefits of building a great America. It is time to stop kidding ourselves about what we need to do in America to be fair and equitable.

Affirmative Action is an American solution. We should be proud that we created and implemented it. It has also been a very successful tool. Evidence of its success lies in the fact that South Africa has imported it. In fact, South Africa is just now starting to use our approach to Civil Rights and Affirmative Action. But, in America, it is time to enhance and/or replace Affirmative Action with a more robust and up-to-date solution.

### *Does Desegregation Still Belong To The Strategy To Improve Black And White Relations?*

Desegregation scared the heck out of many Americans, and I don't know why! Today in America we segregate ourselves based on our music, eating, and worship habits. It does not matter how we developed these preferences. We rally with those who are most like us.

**Music**: We love to live with people who look like us and think like us. Black Americans like loud rhythmic music and voracious preaching in their worship services. Black music is being accepted as a part of mainstream American music. White Americans are starting to enjoy rhythmic music. Most of the gospel musicians I like are White, but they have a very soulful sound. In fact, Black musicians inspired many.

**Worship**: Black Americans like loud preaching. White Americans still do not like loud preaching on a constant basis.

**Food**: Black Americans love tasty food. Traditional Black food has a well-earned reputation for being delicious, but not very healthy. Although White Americans like tasty food, many of them select food that is healthy first and tasty second. That White American food has influenced Black American cuisine is evident in a recent maincourse adaptation: Black Americans now prepare chicken without saturated fat additives.

Although we Americans continue to segregate ourselves based on social status, beliefs, and preferences, color and race is less frequently the reason for segregation. Examples of this promising trend lie in the two places where I am currently living, Portland, Oregon and Boise, Idaho. In Portland, neighborhoods are more clearly divided along racial and ethnic lines. Most Black Americans live in the northeast part of the city. In Boise, there is no section of town that really is a so-called, Black neighborhood. Boise does not have a significant population of Black Americans, and this may be one of the reasons that racial segregation doesn't seem to exit in neighborhoods.

Desegregation was an effective tool in equalizing kindergarten through twelfth grade education. Many Americans had a hard time accepting it. Black and White America learned a lot from this program – and then re-segregated in the south! People want to go to school and church in the neighborhoods where they live. They want to go with people they feel most comfortable with and, most of all, who look like they do. The re-segregation of America happened, because neighborhoods were already segregated on the bases of social economics, ethnic/cultural experiences, and skin color. Therefore, although desegregation was effective in the past, it is no longer so.

## *Are There Other Solutions To Tear Down The Walls Between White And Black America?*

The number of solutions to improve interracial relationships is endless. We Americans are problem-solvers, and we thrive on challenge at work. However, we struggle to find time to solve problems with our people systems. There are many possible solutions to make Black and White American relationships successful – we just need to decide to create and implement them. If each of us faces the challenge of solving a few of the little problems involving race relations, we will tear down the walls of enmity that separate Black and White Americans.

## *Can We Deprogram Black And White America About Black Americans?*

Years of suffering and hatred between White and Black Americans has driven us so far apart that the riff seems that it can never be bridged.But we can bridge it. We must continue to employ a deprogramming process. The way we perceive each other is reflected in how we treat each other. I consider myself to be a tool in deprogramming White Americans on an individual basis. I work hard to be perceived as equal to White Americans, regardless of whether they want me as an equal or not. (Some White Americans when dealing with this line of reasoning become very uncomfortable, even though very few rational White Americans want to be perceived as a racist. In fact, very few White Americans are racist. I believe most White Americans unconsciously practice Racism. I believe most White Americans want to be fair to all Americans! In America, we are challenged by such great obstacles and look forward to finding and implementing solutions.) Presenting myself as their equal helps them see other Black people and me as equal. It is subtle, but effective. Similarly, many other Blacks are presenting themselves as equals to Whites at school and on the job. This has helped to build their self-esteem and helped White people develop a higher esteem for them.

One final assignment: My challenge to each of you is to meet with a Black person this week. During the meeting, tell yourself silently that this person is your equal. You may have had different experiences, have different preferences, and different aptitudes, but you are equal. Try to learn something new about the person. During and after the meeting, examine yourself for any racist thoughts. Recognizing you have such thoughts will help you overcome them. Make the assignment iterative if necessary. You are the hope for all of us in America. The solution starts with you deciding to make the solution a priority.

# Chapter
# 20

## Chapter Twenty - Can White And Black Americans Continue To Live Together

ᵞes! We really don't have much choice. We don't want a choice. We have lived together in this country for over three hundred years. We have not learned to enjoy each other as much as we should have, but we have made progress.

The groundwork for this progress actually started when Pilgrims arrived in America as a result of religious persecution. Tolerance, the American Solution, started at that point. Today, religious persecution is dead in America. We are close to achieving tolerance for racial problems. This is one of the last frontiers of American societal problems.

Futurist and author David Snyder says, we are in a wave of "Creative Destruction!" David didn't give a crisp definition of creative destruction, but what it means to me is that we are very busy creating technology faster than we can learn to use it. We are creating stuff so fast that we are obsoleting what we just created yesterday by what we are creating today, before we have gotten the full value or use out of what we just created yesterday. As the 20th Century closes, America is number one in everything. Our post-industrial boom economy has benefited from technological developments, which, in turn, have yielded an even healthier economy. Our outlook is rosy, but for one potential problem – the inequity Black Americans face. This alone could undo our success. Another incident such as the Rodney King beating or O.J. Simpson trial could prove to be a time bomb.

Perhaps this creative-destructive process is more promising than what we had in the past due to the improvement gained, but we had better start to capitalize on all this creativity. In my opinion, we are on the verge of repeating history by recreating many of the problems we have already solved. To a certain extent, this should not be too scary. Instead, re-solving the same problems may give us opportunities to improve the previous solutions. The art and science of improving, developing newer and better versions, is part of the American way. The glitch is that we must make sure we arrive at a complete solution for Black and White Race Relations, before we decide to review the problem from the beginning.

### *What Do White Americans Need To Know About Black Americans?*

They are a vital part of the American Dream, the American solution and American success!

They will require their rightful place in America.

They are asking for equity and fairness in social economics.

They want sustainable systems built with their success in mind.

They want their history told, understood and honored.

They want respect and acknowledgement based on their significant contribution and participation in the building of America.

They want the difference in their thinking acknowledged, not defamed, because it is different.

They want their accomplishments in areas beyond sports and entertainment acknowledged and valued.

They want the assimilation process to work beyond the color of their skin. For example, Assimilate Black culture into White? Desegregate churches ?

They want their talent valued in the business world.

They want the "System" to treat them fairly.

They want White Americans to take the time to understand the needs of Black Americans, and allow them to create their own solutions.

They want the world to know they are not angry with people, but angry at the inequities of American society.

They want to hold onto some of the things they treasure as "Black." These things should not become levers to separate Black and White Americans.

They want White Americans to understand how the media affects the image of Black Americans and the affect that image has on America.

They want White America to work hard at communicating effectively with Black Americans.

They want White Americans to understand how Racism has evolved and the terrible effects it has on American society.

They want White Americans to know that racial reconciliation is one of the highest priorities of the Black community; it is highly desired at all cost.

They want White Americans to value Black American youth as an important part of America's future.

They want White Americans to continue to evaluate the social programs Black Americans believe they need.

They want White Americans to value Black Americans in the political process.

They want White Americans to understand the importance of the Black Church to the success of the Black community.... and to the success of America.

All of us need to ask ourselves the question that Rodney King posed, "CAN WE ALL GET ALONG?!" And we all need to answer that question, while we aim toward the goal Dr. Martin Luther King put in front of us: "One day all God's Children shall live together free. Free at last, free at last thank God Almighty we are free at last."

Finally, from me to you, we all love America, and we all want America to love us. We all simply want to be Americans! God Bless America!

# Index

# Bibliography

1. The African Origin of Civilization, Cheikh Anta Diop translated from French by Mercer Cook, Lawrence Hill & Co., 1974

2. The Great Fear, By Nine Historians, Edited by Gary B. Nash and Richard Weiss, Holt. Rinehart and Winston, Inc., 1970

3. Black Experience, Strategies and Tactics in the Business World, Darrell D. Simms, Management Aspects Inc., 1991

4. The State of Black America, National Urban League, 1993 The Skanner News Paper, Publisher Bernie Foster, 1996

5. Ebony Magazine, Publisher John H. Johnson, 1996

6. Black Enterprise Magazine, Publisher Earl Graves, 1996

7. Black Heritage Day II, Carl Bernard Mack, 1995

8. The Black Biblical Heritage by John L. Johnson, Winston Derek Publishers, Inc., 1991

9. Beyond The Rivers Of Ethiopia by Mensa Otabil, Pneuma Life Publishers, 1993

10. Black Profiles In Courage by Kareem Abdul-Jabbar and Alan Steinberg, Morrow, 1996

# Order Form

## Requestor's Information:
Name:_____
Address:_____
City:_____State:_____Zip:__
Phone:_____

## Book Order:
May I Help You Understand – ISBN: 0-9630776-7-8
Price: $16.95
Quantity:_____

## Method of Payment:
Visa___ MasterCard____ Exp. Date:_____
Card Holder's Signature:_____
Check No.:_____ (Make Checks Payable to MAI)
Card No._____

## Mail Request To:
Management Aspects Incorporated
16650 SW Heceta Court
Beaverton, OR 97007

## Contact the Publisher:
Phone: 1-877-236-6247(Toll Free)
       1-503-591-0329
E-mail: ma_inc@msn.com